James Joyce

AND THE

COMMON READER

James Joyce

AND THE

COMMON READER

BY WILLIAM POWELL JONES

NORMAN : UNIVERSITY OF OKLAHOMA PRESS

BY WILLIAM POWELL JONES

The Pastourelle: The Origin and Traditions of a Lyric Type (Cambridge, Mass., 1931; New York, 1967)

Thomas Gray, Scholar (Cambridge, Mass., 1937)

Practical Word Study (New York, 1943, 1952)

James Joyce and the Common Reader (Norman, 1955, 1970)

Sawney and Colley and Other Pope Pamphlets (1960)

The Rhetoric of Science: A Study of Scientific Ideas and Imagery in Eighteenth-Century English Poetry (London and Berkeley, 1966)

Acknowledgment is hereby made for permission most generously given to quote from the following works by James Joyce:

Ulysses (copyright 1918, 1919, 1920, by Margaret Caroline Anderson; 1934 by the Modern Library, Inc.; 1942 by Nora Joseph Joyce), by Random House, Inc.

A Portrait of the Artist as a Young Man (copyright 1916 by B. W. Huebsch; 1944 by Nora Joseph Joyce), by The Viking Press, Inc.

Finnegans Wake (copyright 1939 by James Joyce), by The Viking Press, Inc.

INTERNATIONAL STANDARD BOOK NUMBERS:
0–8061–0324–8 (cloth); 0–8061–0930–0 (paper)

LIBRARY OF CONGRESS CATALOG CARD NUMBER: 55–9624

to marian and our four sons

preface to the second printing

Scholarly writings on Joyce have continued to multiply since this book was first published in 1955, and some of them are significant additions to the total picture of the man and his work. Richard Ellmann has published his definitive biography and edited three volumes of letters, and now we have the evidence at first hand of Joyce's lifelong devotion to writing and of the relation of his life to his works. In addition, previously unpublished works by Joyce have appeared: additional pages of *Stephen Hero*, a volume of his critical writings, a fictionalized story of a love affair in Trieste entitled *Giacomo Joyce*, and many excerpts from his notebooks that throw light on the composition of *Ulysses* and *Finnegans Wake*. The flood of critical and scholarly writing about Joyce threatens to inundate even devoted Joyceans.

The reader may then well ask why this little book is still useful. The answer is simple: the book continues to fill the need for a simple guide directly into some of the greatest literature of the twentieth century. For this second printing I have made no changes except to provide a new preface and a new "Advice on Further Reading About Joyce," which comments on the more important recent additions to Joyce scholarship. I could enlarge my analyses of the first three stories of *Dubliners* and some of the episodes in *Ulysses*. I could also do more with *Finnegans Wake*, since the general reader has learned to read small parts of that formidable work with pleasure. But such changes would alter my original purpose, which was to gain more readers for Joyce, especially for *Ulysses*, by explaining his mastery of words and thereby helping the reader enjoy his vivid encyclopedic picture of modern life without too much interference.

The title of my book received some criticism, even though I had defined my "common reader" as one somewhat like Dr. Johnson's, "the intelligent reader who is not a specialist in modern fiction but is willing to work in order to understand any piece of writing that is worth the effort." Joyce scholars, among them Seon Manley, sympathetic to my purposes recognized that I sought to approach the "intelligent reader without artifice but with respect." In a sense, of course, every reader of Joyce is an uncommon reader, but the beginner needs to be shown that he can cut through the difficult symbolism and esoteric criticism (from Joyce himself by way of Stuart Gilbert) to the works themselves. I tried to prove that most of Joyce not only was intelligible to the general reader but could be exciting too.

For the most part the book has been well received and given generous praise for doing what it set out to do. College teachers also found it helpful in introducing Joyce to baffled undergraduates. I have in my files gratifying reviews and letters from many Joyce scholars—Herbert Cahoon, Joseph Remenyi, Joseph Prescott, Richard Ellmann, Richard Kain, James Spoerri, Mitchell Morse, Theodore Spencer, and Margaret Schlauch—and I prize my friendships with them as the greatest reward for my temerity in writing a guide to Joyce.

As I look back, it appears that whatever original contribution I have made to Joyce scholarship proceeded from my interest in linguistics, which first attracted me to *Ulysses*. In 1939, at a meeting of the Modern Language Association, I read a paper in which I analyzed the musical technique of *Finnegans Wake* in terms of Joyce's mastery of words. The linguistic approach to Joyce is of paramount importance, and yet almost no attention has been paid to this aspect of *Ulysses*, and even in *Finnegans Wake* it is, except in the work of Miss Schlauch, generally limited to the obvious. Among the detailed analyses that appeared for the first time in my book are the linguistic analysis of "Oxen of the Sun"; a study of the intentionally inept language of "Eumaeus"; the orgy of Rabelaisian parody in "Cyclops"; the cinematic technique of "Circe"; and the analysis of the linguistic method of *Finnegans Wake*, which includes a full explication of the Bygmester paragraph, as well as of some glorious complicated puns.

Among the comments my book received, one came from an unexpected source, in an article by William Ornstein in *Variety* (June 20, 1962), about producer Jerry Wald's plans to film *Ulysses*. At Wald's request the British director Jack Cardiff studied twelve interpretative volumes on "Joyce's tome," one of which was *James Joyce and the Common Reader*. Afterward, with the help of scriptwriter John McClelland, a scenario was produced that included all eighteen episodes of the novel. The ambitious plans to film the work in Dublin in the fall of 1962 were abandoned on Wald's untimely death. (Five years later *Ulysses* was filmed by Joseph Strick and Fred Haines, who produced a faithful and moving portrayal that aroused heated comment by critics and audiences alike.)

The interesting thing about Wald's plans was his complete dedication to capturing the complexity of the book and the "wonderful rhythm and sound" of the writing. Cinema audiences, Wald said, had rejected the mediocre and expected "something challenging and stimulating." Believing that audiences were "more open and receptive to the new, startling, different, more than ever before in the history of the cinema," he had chosen *Ulysses* as especially adaptable to cinema treatment. For his authority he quoted my analysis of the "Circe" episode, calling attention to the fast-moving scenes in Nighttown, in which the technique is much like that of a well-made modern movie, where "a minimum of talking is supplemented by good directing and skillful photography."

The dramatic quality of the Circe episode was proved by the play *Ulysses in Nighttown*, by Marjorie Barkentin, produced in 1958 at the Rooftop Theatre by Burgess Meredith under the supervision of Padraic Colum. Richard Cordell and Lowell Matson included the play in their *Off-Broadway Theatre* (1959), calling it "easily the boldest and most imaginative off-Broadway achievement in 1958." With a cast of some sixty characters, the play makes use of a narrator and a "mad, feverish ballet" to suggest the subconscious thoughts of Bloom and Stephen. A play was also made from *Portrait of the Artist: Stephen D.*, by Hugh Leonard, in 1963. A dramatization of *Finnegans Wake*, by Mary Manning, was published in 1957. A motion picture of *Finnegans Wake* was produced by Mary Ellen Bute in 1967. Joyce would have approved these dramatic adaptations of his fiction, for he experimented in the cinema himself.

I have resisted the temptation to add to my chapter on *Finnegans Wake*, for it would be dangerous to try to compress in a small book what several book-length guides have not always agreed upon. I have shown how an ordinary reader can make his own interpretations of the daring neologisms and thereby have fun with the great riddle of Haroun Childeric Eggeberth, or Everyman in Dublin. If the reader enjoys the process, he may want to continue it throughout the book. No doubt the readers of *Finnegans Wake* will continue to increase, and each of them will add his own explications until the sum total becomes prodigious. Meanwhile, I had better stick to my original intent: "to show the ordinary reader that, artistically, *Finnegans Wake* is the logical culmination of the two qualities of Joyce's writing that interested me most in *Ulysses*, his mastery of words and his facility in comic satire."

Parts of this book were published in the process of composition. An early version of Chapter IV appeared as "The Common Reader and James Joyce's *Ulysses*" in *The American Scholar* (Spring, 1952) and parts of Chapters VII and VIII as "James Joyce: Master of Words" in the first number of an ill-fated Cleveland literary magazine, *Intersection* (Spring, 1953). As I mentioned above, I read a paper on Joyce's use of musical technique at a meeting of the Modern Language Association in New Orleans in 1939. When I commenced writing the book, I had lectured on Joyce at Toronto (1947), Cornell (1948), and Michigan (1953) as a visiting lecturer from Western Reserve University. In recent years I have given many lectures on Joyce, notably at the Rowfant Club and at the Cleveland Museum of Art.

On all these and other occasions I profited from many critics who listened and questioned and helped me refine my ideas. Joseph Prescott, of Wayne University, contributed his time and his great knowledge of Joyce far beyond the demands of friendship. Howard Allen, my colleague at Western Reserve University, encouraged me to write the book and made valuable suggestions.

Permission to quote from the copyrighted works of James Joyce was given generously, and I remain deeply indebted to the individual publishers of his works.

William Powell Jones

Gates Mills, Ohio
January 15, 1970

contents

James Joyce

AND THE

COMMON READER

CHAPTER ONE

JOYCE IN DUBLIN

James Joyce is much talked about but too little read for a writer of his importance. Those who read him find it hard to judge his work calmly. Some praise him with enthusiasm, while others denounce him as a charlatan. Some say he is playing a gigantic hoax on a credulous public, while others regard him as the most sincere artist and the most influential writer of the twentieth century. Nearly all who seriously read him agree that he is a master of the English language, even when they deplore the things he writes about.

The truth can be found in reconciling all these points of view. Joyce was so concerned with his serious purpose of presenting modern life in terms of the city of Dublin that he never deviated from it. All during his life he kept adding to the picture with the determined zeal of a homesick exile. By the time he finished *Ulysses* in 1922 at the height of his literary career, he had perfected his startling technique well enough to enable him to pack an encyclopedic picture of complicated modern life within the covers of one book. That is a great feat, whether the picture be perfect or not, but it makes hard reading because the book is compact.

Add to this compactness Joyce's increasing concern with his medium, the English language, and the result is to heap novelty upon inventive genius until the quandary of *Finnegans Wake* is reached. But those who would ridicule this last work of the linguistic experimenter should remember that Joyce began with the plain language of the realist in *Dubliners,* added the tortured thoughts of the budding poet in *A Portrait of the Artist as a Young Man,*[1] and reached the height of artistic maturity in *Ulysses* by an infinite variety of new styles, strikingly original but all built on a vocabulary that most of us use and easily understand. Only in *Finnegans Wake* does Joyce change his medium and leave conventional English to build a new and strange vocabulary by miraculous and monstrous blends of English and other languages.

Many intelligent readers have shied away from Joyce because they plunged first into *Ulysses* and became quickly discouraged. If they had started with *Dubliners* and *Portrait of the Artist,* they would have enjoyed the keen observation of life and the exciting but plain language of one of our best writers of modern realistic fiction. They would also have become familiar with the setting and many of the actual characters later used in *Ulysses.* They would know, too, the whole early story of that young intellectual, Stephen Dedalus, whose mental convolutions obscure many pages of Part I of *Ulysses.* They would realize that *Ulysses* was meant to follow *Portrait of the Artist,* not only in its story but especially in the artist's purpose of portraying the universal in terms of the particular or, more precisely, the riddle of modern man in terms of the moral history of Dublin. Realizing all this, the intelligent general reader will be more eager to put forth an extra effort to understand *Ulysses.* He will laugh at the incidental comedy that relieves the larger picture of despair. He will learn to admire

[1] All future references will give the shortened title, *Portrait of the Artist.*

Joyce's skill with words and new styles. And an exciting adventure it will be.

Joyce was twenty-two when he left Ireland in 1904 to spend the rest of his life in voluntary exile writing about what he had experienced in those early years. For thirty-six years, until his death in 1941, he lived in Trieste, Rome, Zurich, Paris, and other parts of the Continent, while he wrote continuously about the one city of Dublin. All his fiction is set in this fervently regional capital of his fervently nationalistic native country. His youthful book of stories, *Dubliners*, was meant, he said, to portray the moral history of Ireland. His autobiographical novel, *Stephen Hero*, became compressed into *Portrait of the Artist*, the story of a young writer's struggles against the harshness of Dublin. His *Ulysses* is the whole history of Dublin concentrated into the wanderings of Leopold Bloom on June 16, 1904. His *Finnegans Wake* exalts Dublin to a universal plane that makes it almost unrecognizable.

This combination of the cosmopolitan and regional is merely a symbol of Joyce's lifelong desire to express the universal history of mankind in terms of the purely local. Joyce himself said that he chose the versatile Ulysses as the model for his complete all-round man in preference to Faust and Hamlet. It may be denied that Leopold Bloom, the Joycean Ulysses, even approaches the complete man; yet the activities of Bloom and his fellow-Dubliners on June 16, 1904, present perhaps as complete a picture of multiform and complicated modern life as can be given within the covers of one book. What the tolerant and compromising Bloom lacks in completeness is more than compensated by other characters in the book: by the intellectual Stephen Dedalus, the sensual Molly Bloom, and the two hundred or more Dubliners of every description and trade and mood who walk boldly into the episodes.

Finnegans Wake, the work that was in progress for seventeen years, pushes to its extreme Joyce's desire to express the universal in terms of the particular. Even when the particulars are unintelligible, the general theme of the book is not hard to follow—that history repeats itself; that life consists of the constantly recurring cycle of birth, marriage, death, and reawakening; and that time does not matter, since the cycle is apparent in Adam and Tristram and Napoleon as well as in H. C. Earwicker, that citizen of Dublin whose dreams are the matter of the book.

It is no accident that Joyce was successful in accomplishing his lifelong desire of expressing the universal in terms of the realistic details of life in Dublin as he knew it when he was growing up. It was part of his aesthetic theory that great writers became international because they were intensely national first. "For myself, I always write about Dublin," he told Arthur Power, "because if I can get to the heart of Dublin I can get to the heart of all the cities of the world. In the particular is contained the universal."[2]

When Joyce was talking to Power, he used Turgenev as an example. He might better have used Tolstoy or, going back to older writers whom he revered and followed, Homer and Dante. The *Odyssey* of Homer became the model for Joyce's universal picture of modern man, and yet the old epic is so packed with realistic details of everyday life in ancient Greece that a modern reader can tell from it just what the food, houses, transportation,

[2] From *The Old Waterford House* (London, Mellifont Press, n.d.), 64.

sports, amusements, weapons, and even baths were like in Greece around 1000 B.C. Dante used real people as examples of his vast ethical scheme and wrote the symbolism of his Hell, Purgatory, and Paradise in terms of metaphors describing the countryside and the customs of thirteenth-century Italy. Dante is indeed so lavish with the particulars that his universal picture of man's progress in *The Divine Comedy* is a medieval encyclopedia that serves as model for Joyce's encyclopedia of modern life in *Ulysses*.

The dedicated purpose of the artist is reflected in Joyce's lifelong concern with this depicting of the history of mankind in terms of the city he loathed and loved. The achievement of the artist is reflected in the tremendous impact of his writing upon modern literature. Joyce has long been recognized by writers and serious critics everywhere, until he is now glibly labeled by many "the writer's writer." At the same time some intelligent readers have been unwilling to forgive Joyce for the obscurity that often comes from his continual concern with his medium, his desire to push the boundaries of language farther and farther from the conventional style he inherited. The critic is well aware that from time to time the linguistic experimenter in Joyce has submerged the artist. The ordinary reader, on the other hand, at first sees all as obscure and instinctively refuses to go along on the daring flights.

Still it is for the ordinary reader that this book is written, to analyze the increasing degree of experimentation that Joyce used in developing his universal theme. This has been done in order that those who have not experienced the delights of reading Joyce may come to understand what he is trying to do and at the same time, in the very process of trying to understand, enjoy what is worth all the extra effort it takes to enjoy it. Those who read Joyce with understanding will see the pity and terror in the picture of modern man in all his hopes and despair. At the same time they can feast on the mastery of English style and on the abundant comedy and rollicking satire so often overlooked. In this book the major effort is on *Ulysses*, because it is, in my opinion, his mature masterpiece. It is fuller and therefore more difficult than his earlier work, yet it is still within the conventional limits of the English language and therefore much more easily understood than *Finnegans Wake*. We must nevertheless begin with Joyce as a young artist in order to see how he develops the story of man in terms of the people of Dublin, from the realistic sketches in *Dubliners* to the daring experimentation of *Finnegans Wake*.

CHAPTER TWO

ÒUBLIПΣRS:
OR THE MORAL HISTORY OF IRELAND

Joyce began his writing with realistic stories about familiar things around him, but before the stories were published in *Dubliners* he had developed the idea of arranging them in a pattern that would depict the "moral history of Ireland," as he called it. From that time all his work might well be entitled "Everyman in Dublin," for he used the same setting and many of the same characters in his variations of the story of all mankind.

Beginning with *Dubliners*, therefore, we can see how his later themes are boldly outlined in his earlier works, how he progressed gradually in his broad project. It has long been recognized by critics that Joyce thought of all his writing as being the development of one large story, that his two early books contain characters and scenes that appear later in *Ulysses*, that his *Portrait of the Artist* is the spiritual biography of the Stephen Dedalus who brings many of his youthful companions with him into *Ulysses*, and that *Ulysses* was planned as a sequel to the earlier *Portrait of the Artist*. Only in recent years, however, has further study demonstrated just how carefully this was planned by Joyce, how *Dubliners* was planned as a "moral history of Ireland" long before *Ulysses*, and how Joyce's real autobiography, recently published in part as *Stephen Hero*, suffered a sea change until it came out in his *Portrait of the Artist* as the picture of the young intellectual who was very different from Joyce.

The first step in the progression is the series of stories known as Dubliners. When Joyce left Dublin on October 8, 1904, to live the rest of his life on the Continent, he had already begun his autobiographical *Stephen Hero* and written some of the stories for *Dubliners*. During the next year he relieved the tedium of teaching at the Berlitz School in Trieste by completing the stories that formed the original idea of *Dubliners* as well as writing over nine hundred pages of *Stephen Hero* and preparing his first book of poems, *Chamber Music*, for publication. On October 15, 1905, he wrote to publisher Grant Richards that *Dubliners* was ready and should be "commercial" since books on cities and on Irish subjects were then popular. The disheartening story of Joyce's attempts to publish the book, unsuccessful until nine years later, does not belong here, but the author's attempt to justify his first important work throws considerable light on his aims in writing *Dubliners*.[1]

The fourteen stories that make up the original book (excluding the long story, "The Dead," written in 1907 and added in the 1914 edition) are realistic sketches of life as Joyce saw it in Dublin during his youth. They are very easy to read, for the language is plain, the characters are portrayed with amazing compression and the peculiar rhythm of Irish speech is reproduced faithfully. They would, in fact, require no comment except for the fact that a careful reading of them shows Joyce's development as a serious artist. They furnish clear proof that as early as 1904 he was intent

[1] Herbert Gorman, *James Joyce* (New York, Rinehart Publishing Company, 1939, 145–74.

on showing the universal in terms of the particular city he knew best, and that the conciseness with which he succeeds in carrying out this serious purpose in *Dubliners* is no accident.

When the "moral British printer" frowned on portions of *Dubliners* that now seem innocent, Joyce wrote publisher Grant Richards several long and rather heated rebuttals in which his artistic purpose is carefully expressed. He summed it up best in the letter of May 5, 1906: "My intention was to write a chapter of the moral history of my country and I chose Dublin for the scene because that city seemed to me the centre of paralysis. I have tried to present it to the indifferent public under four of its aspects: childhood, adolescence, maturity, and public life. The stories are arranged in this order. I have written it for the most part in a style of scrupulous meanness and with the conviction that he is a very bold man who dares to alter in the presentment, still more to deform, whatever he has seen and heard." This last statement reminds us of Chaucer (mentioned in the same letter), who once warned his readers that he had to write everything as he saw it or else falsify his material, and that if they were squeamish about ribald stories they had better turn over the leaf and choose another. Without considering the question of morals in realism, however, let us look at the material in *Dubliners* in the light of the artist's professed purpose.

The fourteen stories in the original series are quite realistic sketches of people in Dublin of all ages and all phases of life, each sketch a sort of slice of life that makes a comment on the "moral history" of mankind without moralizing. They are not "short stories" in the usual definition of that genre. Without traditional plot structure each story presents a central character or group of characters in a frustrating situation, but in each sketch the reader must finish the story for himself in his own mind. The technique was already known in the stories of Chekhov, and since Joyce it has become so well known in the stories of Katherine Mansfield and *The New Yorker* magazine that no one finds it unusual now.

Even in the very plain language of this early work, however, Joyce realized that he could never completely tell the story of modern man and so he was trying in these sketches merely to suggest, by certain well-chosen characters in one supreme reveal-ing moment of their chaotic lives, the hidden meaning of compli-cated modern life. Joyce thinks of the story as a sudden moment of insight, a revelation like that to Paul on the road to Damascus, an "epiphany" like that of the divinity of Christ appearing to the Three Wise Men in the stable at Bethlehem. "By epiphany," Joyce lets the younger writer say in *Stephen Hero*, "he meant a sudden spiritual manifestation, whether in the vulgarity of speech or of gesture or in a memorable phase of the mind itself. He be-lieved it was for the man of letters to record these epiphanies with extreme care, seeing that they themselves are the most delicate and evanescent of moments."

These revealing moments or "epiphanies" appear more and more concisely in Joyce's later writings, when the artist realized that he could never express all the despair and hope in man's wanderings through life in the modern world. More and more he resorts to "a memorable phase of the mind itself," the so-called stream of consciousness, because it is more compact and poignant in its revealing. But the germ and the desire are already present in the stories of *Dubliners*, and the epiphany is here the more understandable to the common reader because the moment, sudden and compressed though it may be, is still described in conventional and plain language and is more concerned with speech and gesture than with the mind.

The original fourteen stories of *Dubliners* follow roughly the scheme outlined by Joyce in the letter to his publisher already quoted. Even a cursory analysis will show, however, that the stories do not fall into a neat series of three or four stories to each category, and certainly not into the elaborate symbolistic parallels with Homer's *Odyssey* recently suggested by Richard Levin and Charles Shattuck.[2] The wanderer in Dublin is the artist himself, observing the characters that symbolize the moral history of Ireland, but evidence that Joyce had already conceived the idea of picturing the universal hero in terms of Ulysses-Bloom is not convincing.

A brief analysis of the stories will show what I mean. Childhood and adolescence are briefly portrayed in the first three stories, where the inner life of a boy's mind is revealed so sharply and sympathetically that the stories seem to belong to the autobiographical *Stephen Hero* that Joyce was writing at the same time. They are culled out and put here because they are moments illustrating a more universal theme than that of the artist as a young man.

[2] *James Joyce: Two Decades of Criticism* (New York, Vanguard Press, 1948), 47–94. Joyce looked on Ulysses as a favorite hero even when he was a boy, and we know that he contemplated in 1907 writing another story for *Dubliners* based on a modern Ulysses wandering through Dublin but never got any farther than the title because the germinating idea was even then growing into the later *Ulysses*. The parallels cited in this ingenious study are unconvincing: the boy in the first three stories is nothing like Telemachus, and the mature characters of the rest of the book would have to change shapes oftener than Proteus himself to be like Homer's Odysseus.

The next group is the "meat" of the book, eight stories of grown men and women who are certainly old enough to be mature even if they do not always act like adults. The last group of three stories represents public life in Ireland, as the characters in turn portray politics, art, and religion—three subjects that assume gigantic roles in Joyce's later work. The added story, "The Dead," although it does not belong to the original series, fits in very well with the last two categories of maturity and public life. Its many characters are realistically set in the background of Irish music and hospitality, with comments on Irish politics and religion added. Finally, as if for good measure, Joyce includes in "The Dead" a new theme, that of mature love sympathetically portrayed. The geniality and warmth of this story, in spite of its title, seem to have been intended by the author to lift the collection from that "special odour of corruption" which earlier he had boasted the stories had. The artist is himself growing up to the maturity and sympathy of *Ulysses*.

A more detailed analysis of *Dubliners* shows how the stories fit the scheme of childhood, adolescence, maturity, and public life—terms that Joyce used to explain the book. The following descriptions of the themes of the stories, brief though they are, should reveal the artist's purpose and his reasons for insisting that publishers follow exactly the order in which he had arranged his "epiphanies." The scheme appears to be simple enough, yet it shows Joyce's concern with his main purpose in his earliest work. The importance of mature Dubliners in the picture of modern man seems obvious here, but I have not seen it described in any criticism of Joyce.

Childhood.
> "The Sisters." A boy's first experience with death.
> "An Encounter." A sensitive boy's first encounter with the sordid world.

Adolescence.
> "Araby." Puppy love of a boy for an older woman.

Maturity. Eight stories arranged in four apparently contrasting pairs, the ages of the chief characters increasing to late middle age, or roughly from twenty to forty.

> *Contrasting attitudes toward family responsibility by mature young people.*
>> "Eveline." Young woman gives up a romantic dream to resume a drab domestic situation.
>> "After the Race." Young man finds excitement only in wasting his father's money.

> *Contrasting attitudes toward illicit love affairs.*
>> "Two Gallants." Egotistical reprobate makes good his boast of power over a servant girl who loves him.
>> "The Boarding House." Circumspect young man is tricked into marriage by a scheming mother.

> *Contrasting attitudes toward the frustrating responsibilities of family life.*
>> "A Little Cloud." Meek little man, reminded of his thwarted career as a writer, rebels for a moment against his wife but quickly changes when he be-

comes aware of the greater strength of her maternal fury.

"Counterparts." Handsome man, frustrated by the growing burden of his large family and by the demands of his irascible employer, seeks the solace of carousing on borrowed money and finally shows his cowardice by beating the son who sat up to cook his dinner.

Contrasting situations of two celibates in late middle age.

"Clay." Middle-aged spinster, on a visit to a family she knows well, shows her domestic instincts in many ways, especially in her love for the children of her friends.

"A Painful Case." Middle-aged bachelor breaks off a Platonic love affair with a married woman, causing her death.

Public life. Three stories centering about Irish politics, art, and religion.

"Ivy Day in the Committee Room." Contrast between sordid ward politics and the fine spirit of Parnell, the Irish leader.

"A Mother." Devastating picture of an overbearing woman who calculated her own marriage and now tries to run her daughter's life as well as her singing career.

"Grace." Attempted regeneration of a once highly reputable salesman who has fallen to the lowest stages of irresponsible drunkenness.

Epilogue combining maturity and public life (added to original scheme).

> "The Dead." Long story, twice the length of the longest of the other stories in *Dubliners*, involving many characters in the setting of a private musical concert. Politics, religion, and music are fully commented on, while Irish hospitality is also described. The action centers on Gabriel and Gretta Conroy, who relive scenes from the past under the stimulation of the music and the festivity. While the theme of the story is a "man's withdrawal into the circle of his own egotism,"[3] the longing of Gabriel for his wife is a reflection of mature married love, a theme untouched in the earlier stories. With the introduction of the boy who died romantically for love of Gretta at the age of seventeen, the theme of mutual love of man and wife is temporarily interrupted but in the end appears to have been strengthened.

Joyce's steady insistence that his publishers keep this order for the tales in *Dubliners* now appears to have had good artistic motivation. The only explanation he gave, so far as I can discover, was that he was portraying the moral history of Ireland in the order of childhood, adolescence, maturity, and public life. Let us follow this scheme with a more detailed analysis.

The first three stories have in common the same general theme of a sensitive boy reacting for the first time to some im-

[3] David Daiches, *The Novel and the Modern World*, containing an excellent analysis of "The Dead," (Chicago, University of Chicago Press, 1939), 91–100.

portant experience. The boy tells his stories in the first person. He takes care not to give his name, though we know he must be close kin to, if not actually, Stephen Dedalus. In fact, the stories could easily have been episodes in the autobiographical novel, *Stephen Hero*, that Joyce was beginning to write about the same time.

The author does not tell the boy's age, but in "Araby" he seems older than in the first two stories. In "The Sisters," he is old enough to be angry with Old Cotter for alluding to him as a child, and in "An Encounter," he is old enough to risk a day away from school and wise enough to beware of the old man's advances. In both stories, however, the boy is still responding as a youngster. In the first story, he has to be urged to enter the room where the corpse of his friend lies, and his reaction combines boyish horror at death with a sympathetic understanding of the tragic life of the old priest. In the second story, the enthusiasm for reading Wild West stories, the desire to join the others in playing hooky from school, and the first naïve response to the sinister old man —all these, enriched with illustrative detail, describe a young boy's mind better than do the first episodes of *Portrait of the Artist*.

The boy in "Araby" is older than in the first two stories, older in experience if not in years. His adolescent puppy love for Mangan's sister becomes fervent in contrast to the indifference of the older woman as she humors him with casual conversation about a bazaar called Araby. His resentment against the tedious work of school because it stands between him and desire like "ugly monstrous child's play," his anger directed at his uncle for treating him like a child, and finally his frustration at discovering that the adult world he expected to find in the bazaar is empty and cheerless—these are the marks of an adolescent who is sniffing manhood but knows in his heart that he is still a boy and is unhappy because of it.

All the remaining stories in *Dubliners* are about adults, but if we exclude the last four, for reasons already given, the eight stories from "Eveline" to "A Painful Case" represent a very compact artistic group. They not only depict "maturity" in Joyce's scheme, but they also treat varied and contrasting points of view towards mature life so carefully that the order in which they appear assumes unusual significance. Although I have tried to indicate this artistic balance in the outline of *Dubliners*, a more detailed analysis will illustrate the point.

In the first pair of stories, the main characters are young adults placed in a situation that will test their attitude towards *social and family responsibility*. The two main characters and their situations are so different, however, that the contrast more than doubles the author's comment on the theme. Eveline at nineteen is much more adult than is Jimmy Doyle at twenty-six, and so age does not matter much. Eveline had to work hard, during the day as a store clerk and the rest of the time as housekeeper for two men and mother of two children. Frank represented the only fun she had known, and she was excited at the prospect of leaving her drab home and going to Buenos Aires with him. But at the last minute, "like a helpless animal," she refused to go. Jimmy in "After the Race" is just the opposite, a carefree and gay young man who has never grown up. He recklessly spends the profits from his father's butcher shops because he likes the excitement of being associated with sporting foreigners. Jimmy loses heavily at gambling, excited because he thinks he is seeing life when he is accepted as an equal by European racers and an American millionaire. We feel the mad race will go on forever, for Jimmy will never assume any responsibilities.

The next pair of stories contains a contrast, not only in character and theme but also in plot structure. In "Two Gallants," Corley and Lenehan are both lecherous by nature, but Corley is the brash, confident, amoral libertine who is so successful that the servant girl who gives him her love also gives him money, while Lenehan, tired of the world at the age of thirty-one, enviously wishes for "some good simple-minded girl with a little of the ready." In "The Boarding House," on the other hand, Mr. Doran had settled down to a respectable business career, when at thirty-five he was taken in by the advances of nineteen-year-old Polly, daughter of his boardinghouse keeper. The scheming mother let Polly flirt with other young men but she cleverly blackmailed Mr. Doran, fearful of scandal, into marrying Polly for his one indiscretion. The aggressor in both stories gets what he or she wants, while the victim, though by no means innocent, is punished far more than she or he deserves, and so each of them arouses our sympathy.

The next pair of stories presents two totally dissimilar fathers who have in common the feeling that the responsibilities of family life have frustrated them completely. The manner in which each meets the given situation is as different as can be. In "A Little Cloud" the reunion of Little Chandler with his successful journalist friend from London reminds him vividly that he should have been a poet instead of a drab clerk. He goes home thinking of his frustration but he sees the responsibilities of home life so sympathetically that he forgets about escape. The frantic crying of his baby and the skillful way his wife handles the situation make him ashamed of having thought of rebellion.

In "Counterparts" the opposite is true. Farrington is about as near a villain as Joyce ever created. We may sympathize with his rebellion against the drabness of his copyist job and the seeming tyranny of his employer, but soon we realize that Farrington is much to blame even there. The humiliations and frustrations grow, however, and in his weak way he finds solace only in drink. He is further humiliated before his companions in a test of physical strength with a mere boy. When he goes home, late at night, sullen and angry, and savagely beats the son who has waited up to get supper for him, we cannot forgive him. We remember sensitive Chandler with tears of remorse because he had resented his baby's crying, and the contrast Joyce has so vividly created appears in masterful colors.

The last pair of stories in this group of eight involves two lonely celibates who have let life slip by. In "Clay," Maria leaves the cheerless routine of her work at a laundry to visit a home she knows well, and she is happy in the cheer she brings to others. In "A Painful Case," Mr. James Duffy rejects the love of a married friend and finds years later that his act of virtuous renunciation has brought about her suicide and his own unhappiness. The contrast in situations points no moral; it merely accentuates the irony of life. Maria is a spinster who would have made a wonderful mother. The women at the laundry where she works love her because she tries to bring a touch of home life to the drab establishment. The family she visits is her own family for this one evening, and there is no regret except for the youth that has gone.

Mr. James Duffy, on the other hand, is a meticulous bachelor who could bear no "physical or mental disorder." His routine was disturbed by a friendly lady who sat next to him at a concert one night. His friendship with Mrs. Sinico deepened and became intense with time. He warmed to her interest in his writing and selfishly absorbed the passion that he discreetly thought was Platonic. He was very much surprised when one night she "caught up his hand passionately and pressed it to her cheek." They agreed to break off, and four years later he read of her suicide. He now realized that his rectitude had sentenced one who had loved him to a death of shame. Now he was really alone.

The last four stories are also tales of mature people in other aspects of Ireland's moral history, yet they stand apart because they also portray phases of public life and are unified by that theme. The revelation of life in the characters in these stories, however, means much more than the brief pictures they give of Dublin's public life. In "Ivy Day in the Committee Room" the attitude of the political workers towards their great hero Parnell is far more poignant than the picture of Irish ward politics. In "A Mother" the scheming woman who selfishly plots an ambitious musical career for her daughter and overreaches herself in the attempt will linger in the reader's mind longer than Joyce's picture of singing concerts. And in "Grace" the depths of drunken debauchery Joyce uses as prelude to his story of redemption is many times more vivid than the author's comment on Irish religion. Finally, "The Dead" transcends all neat patterns and in fact combines them all into one lengthy and magnificent story. But "The Dead," as we now know, was not written as part of the original scheme of *Dubliners*.

These fifteen stories are a more composite unit than critics have hitherto shown. They are brief moments, it is true—the episodes, or "epiphanies" that portray Joyce's Ireland in terms of the realistic speech and gesture of Dubliners of various ages and many walks of life. But the whole picture is fuller because of the compact arrangement of the stories of mature life in four pairs of contrasting characters and situations, followed by four stories, also about mature people, that add a revealing comment on some aspect of Ireland's public life. Joyce carefully planned the arrangement of the stories to carry out his intentions. External action based on real life is still the chief medium rather than the stream of consciousness made famous in *Ulysses*. The stories are the inspired moments that reveal the universal desires of man in terms of the particular Dubliners of all ages whom Joyce parades before us.[4]

[4] Since this was written, Joyce's brother Stanislaus has substantiated my criticism of *Dubliners* in a BBC broadcast printed in *The Listener*, Vol. LI, No. 1308 (March 25, 1954), 526f. He gives many interesting biographical facts that show the genesis of several stories in *Dubliners*. He offers convincing evidence of his brother's writing these stories from real life and dismisses all mystical interpretations. Stanislaus Joyce also points to an "underlying plan" for the book and cites as illustration the grouping of the first three stories as descriptive of adolescent life and of the pair of stories, "A Painful Case" and "Clay," as presenting "types of celibates, male and female."

CHAPTER THREE

THE YOUNG ARTIST IN ᗞUBLIᑎ

Along with *Dubliners,* Joyce was writing a long autobiographical novel, which he called *Stephen Hero,* written in the same plain language and illustrated with the same rich variety of realistic details as the stories in *Dubliners.* But the hero is Stephen Dedalus-James Joyce, and the matter is centered on the actions and the thoughts of this one serious and sensitive young man. As the story progressed and the voluminous manuscript piled up, Joyce saw that he was going to have to select from it if it was ever to be published. More and more the realistic autobiography became the story of a young artist struggling against his environment. Eventually he was ready to publish the new version as *Portrait of the Artist,* but it is only with the posthumous publication of part of the original *Stephen Hero* that we have been able to see clearly the evolution of Stephen Dedalus from the autobiographical novel to his role as part of the picture of universal modern man in *Ulysses.*

The second step in the progress of the theme of universal modern man in Dublin lies in this development of Stephen Dedalus. The actual history of the evolution of this story is now well known. By March 13, 1906, Joyce writes publisher Grant Richards that he has already finished 914 pages of an autobiographical novel, twenty-five chapters running to 150,000 words, but he is still only half done and unable at that time "to think the rest of the book much less to write it." In 1908 he destroyed part of the novel in a fit of despair and started over, compressing the realistic *Stephen Hero* into the more introspective work that from 1911 definitely bore the title, A *Portrait of the Artist as a Young Man*. The finished work was published serially early in 1914 in *The Egotist* in London, and within the same year *Dubliners* was finally published. Already Joyce was writing *Ulysses*, the book that had been gestating in his mind for many years. It would begin with Stephen Dedalus where *Portrait of the Artist* had left off, but it would be broader in scope until it embraced all people in Dublin instead of the one young artist.

Portrait of the Artist is then the prologue to *Ulysses* and second step in Joyce's artistic scheme of portraying modern man in terms of Dublin, but it is not autobiography. The 300,000 words planned for the autobiographical novel have been compressed into the story of a young writer told in about 75,000 words. A comparison of the finished work with the portion of the original *Stephen Hero* that has survived shows readily the difference in style and point of view.[1] *Stephen Hero* portrays a struggling adolescent, his companions and the members of his family, in the plain language and realistic method used in *Dubliners*. The story, as far as it goes, gives much more detail about the Dedalus family (especially the sick sister, Isabella), recounts fully the sexual attractiveness of Emma Clery, and contains an angry denunciation of

[1] *Stephen Hero, A Part of the First Draft of A Portrait of the Artist as a Young Man*, edited from the manuscript in the Harvard College Library by Theodore Spencer (New York, New Directions, 1944).

the Roman Catholic Church. But Joyce changed his conception of the book, and, as he did so, he became more detached. He not only compressed the realistic details of an adolescent's struggles against his environment, but with the compression he changed the aim, symbolized in the new title, to the spiritual evolution of a serious writer who develops a new artistic creed as he revolts against those things in his life that tied him down—his family, his religion, his country, and his fleshly desires. An analysis of *Portrait of the Artist* will show how he does this.

Chapter I.

The *theme* is the importance of childhood and early school-days at Clongowes Wood in forming the artist. Emphasizing the keen sense impressions of the growing child, the chapter provides background for later attitudes on family, religion, and politics.

The *style* is mostly realistic for the chapter is full of incidents like those in *Dubliners*, moments that reveal the sensitive boy who listens. Yet even here there is a prophecy of the stream-of-consciousness style as the future poet is partially revealed in terms of the thoughts of the boy commenting on what he takes in through the senses. Examples of acute sense impressions are abundant: smells like the odor of his mother and father, the smell of urine on an oilsheet, the smell of peasants ("air and rain and turf and corduroy"), the cold night smell of a chapel, the smell of wine on a priest's breath at first communion; sounds, ugly like the "suck" of dirty water let out of a washbasin, beautiful like the sound of cricket bats ("pick, pack, pock, puck; like drops of water in a fountain falling softly in the brimming bowl"); touch, like that of the cold slime of a ditch or of the prefect's cold hands on his feverish brow, which reminds him of rats with sleek, slimy coats and black, shining eyes; sight, like the earth in geography lessons, a big green ball in maroon clouds, or like the Christmas colors of red holly and green ivy; taste, like that of the turkey and ham and celery and plum pudding of Christmas dinner. The realism is made keener, even in boyhood, by passages dominated by imagination, the stream of consciousness that becomes more prominent as the book progresses. For example, as Stephen lies feverish in bed, a ghost story becomes in his mind a vivid picture of "marshals who had received their death wound on battlefields far away over the sea." In the same infirmary episode he imagines himself being buried—the scene is full of pomp and sadness and beauty, and he wants to cry not for himself but for the beautiful, sad words of an old song. Before Stephen has recovered, he is reminded by the flickering of fire on a wall of waves that in turn call up the sorrowful face of Brother Michael addressing a multitude of people about Parnell, and that reminds him of home.

Episodes (epiphanies):

Miscellaneous impressions of Stephen's early childhood. Various scenes around school culminate in illness at the infirmary (1–26).

Realistic scene of the Christmas party at home, where the impression of prosperity and hospitality is interrupted by a frantic and vociferous quarrel between members of the household over the Church and the Irish patriot Parnell (26–41).

Series of school scenes where Stephen struggles valiantly and with partial success against the bullying of unsympathetic schoolmates and the tyranny of Jesuit discipline. The high points are two scenes in which Stephen's brutal and unfair treatment by Father Dolan is contrasted with his kindly treatment by the rector, Father Conmee. Father Arnall, gentle though strict, represents the middle ground of futile compassion (41–61).

Chapter II.

The *theme* is Stephen's change and growth through a variety of experiences: from childhood to adolescence, from Blackrock to Dublin, from Clongowes school to Belvedere, from romantic love to purchased sexual solace.

The *style* is similar to that of Chapter I but places growing emphasis on the boy's mental reactions to external happenings.

Episodes:

Nostalgic pictures of Stephen's idyllic life at the early home he is about to leave: walks with Uncle Charles and glimpses of the adult world that seems drawing near, for which he must get ready; reading romances and building from them a dream world of his own that includes a Mercedes who is not even aware that she is his love; adventures with a rough boy, Aubrey Mills (compare the boy's companion of "The Encounter" in *Dubliners*). The key to this epiphany is in the boy's brooding upon the image of Mercedes, imagining himself transfigured as they stood alone: "Weakness and timidity and inexperience would fall from him in that magic moment" (65–71).

Sharply realistic scenes from new life in Dublin and at Belvedere College accentuate Stephen's disillusionment over the weakness of his father and the unfriendly school life. The move to Dublin with its cheerless house sends him embittered around the new city, where he notes with vague dissatisfaction the vast variety of the city that is from now on to be the scene of all his writing—its docks, carts, and bales of merchandise, even the ill-dressed, bearded policeman. Angry at being young and having to face the squalor of the new world shaping up, Stephen pretends to chronicle with patience and detachment what he sees. Meanwhile, his love life progresses, for the visionary Mercedes gives way to a real girl; he wants to kiss her, but instead goes home to write a poem in which he does kiss her. The boys at school tease him in admiration of his prowess with the ladies; they admire him for his ability to act and to imitate the rector, but they do not hesitate to torment him for not confessing that Byron was no good. Stephen feels happy only when he is far from his schoolmates; he rebels against them and his family. "Cast down by the dull phenomenon of Dublin," he spends his spare time reading "subversive writers" who set up a ferment in his brain. He reflects on doing many decent things, such as taking part in the Irish national revival or working to restore the family fortunes, but he rejects these phantoms. His rebellion is symbolized at the end of the episode by his ignoring his admiring family after a successful theatrical performance and walking at breakneck speed through the streets until "wounded pride and fallen hope and baffled desire" disappear, and he becomes calm again (71–96).

Vividly realistic scenes of a trip taken by Stephen and his father to Cork where family property is to be sold at auction. Here the family tradition of good fellowship and "manliness" is shown in the pictures of his father's tremendous extrovert masculinity and his grandfather's reputation with women. The reminder causes a faint sickness in Stephen as he recalls his own position at school, "proud and sensitive and suspicious, battling against the squalor of his life and against the riot of his mind." The virility of Simon Dedalus mocks the boy's "bodily weakness and futile enthusiasms." He now knows that he is separated from his father by "an abyss of fortune or of temperament." After this realization he feels completely lost, with nothing stirring within him but a cold and loveless lust (97–108).

Stephen attempts to find "order and elegance" by spending his prize money on lavish gifts for his family, but when his money has been all spent his futile isolation becomes more apparent than ever. In the final scene of this rebellious and unhappy chapter, Stephen turns to savage physical desire as an outlet. For a moment he appears to have found peace in his surrender to a whore. (108–14).

Chapter III.

The *theme* of this chapter, sin followed by remorse, repentance, and final redemption, is in one frantic and frightening episode.

The *style*, dictated by the boy's mental agony, is dominantly that of the stream of consciousness, made more poignant by the seemingly objective reporting of two sermons that are masterpieces of emotional oratory. This long epiphany, a revelation in almost the religious sense of the word, depicts a crisis in Stephen's life. It begins with avid pursuit of the sensual pleasures to which he has yielded, prowling for a "sudden call to his sin-loving soul" from the soft, perfumed flesh of the whores. The very thought of the religious devotions which he has renounced reminds him of the lewd kisses, and the heavy burden of the sins leads him nearer in his imagination to "the refuge of sinners," the Blessed Virgin

Mary. He attends a Jesuit retreat lasting three days, which is described in great detail. The sermons describe vividly the terrors of the last judgment and the horrible punishment awaiting sinners, even to the rain that, falling noiselessly, will rise until it covers the earth and chokes off all life. The final sermon reiterates the tortures of Hell, physical and spiritual, stretching out into eternity, the mere thought of which makes the brain reel dizzily. The sermon ends with an emotional call to repentence that would do credit to an evangelist. The effect of all this on the sensitive boy's imagination is overwhelming. He kneels beside his bed, trying to find a way back to grace, but in his mind he sees creatures that remind him of his foul sins of lust, "goatish creatures with human faces, horny browed . . . their long swishing tails besmeared with stale shite, thrusting upwards their terrific faces." After long agony and a restless walk through the dark streets, Stephen seeks a chapel where he can confess his sins. He walks home and sits by the fire in the kitchen, "not daring to speak for happiness." The communion breakfast of white pudding, eggs, sausages, and tea symbolizes the simplicity and beauty of life that now lies all before him.

Chapter IV. ✓

The *theme* is that of Stephen's new life of devotion and contemplation followed by rejection of a call to the priesthood in order to take up the more complete life of the priestly writer.

The *style* is almost completely dominated by stream of consciousness, since the motivation for Stephen's decision is entirely in his own mind. This chapter, a masterpiece of interior monologue, is the high point of the book.

Episodes:

In his new life Stephen strives "to undo the sinful past" by constant mortification, disciplining his senses in ways that require ingenuity; for example, the only odor distasteful to him "was a certain stale fishy stink like that of longstanding urine: and whenever it was possible he subjected himself to this unpleasant odor." He becomes very inventive at mortifying the touch, enduring every itch and pain and carrying his arms stiffly at his sides like a runner (170–78).

The director conveys to Stephen a call to the priesthood. At first he is filled with pride and elation, but, as he thinks it over, he is repelled by the passionless chilliness of the ordered life. During his walk home, he notices the disorder, misrule, and confusion that attract him more. This feeling is emphasized by finding his parents are out looking for a new house since they have been evicted again. Struck by the pain and weariness in life that are yet balanced by hope of better things, Stephen knows he has rejected the priesthood. (178–90).

This epiphany is packed with beauty and precision as the new life develops in the artist's mind. His entering the university symbolizes the break with the past and marks "the first noiseless sundering of his life from his mother's." Anticipation of his new adventure fills him with the exaltation of fitful music and triple-branching flames and wild creatures racing. It is then that Stephen realizes that what goes on in the mind is more important than what happens externally, that words mean more than things, that "the contemplation of an inner world of individual emotions" put into words is more pleasing to him than "the reflection of the glowing sensible world through the prism of a language many-coloured and richly storied." He knows that such a conception of the writer's art will involve daring experimentation, but he takes courage in thinking of Dedalus, the fabulous artificer whose name he bears, a hawklike man flying with the wings he had invented, above the waves and slowly climbing, "a symbol of the artist forging anew in his workshop out of the sluggish matter of the earth a new soaring impalpable imperishable being."

Stephen then walks along the shore of Dublin's tidal waters, even as he does later in *Ulysses*, fashioning in his mind the subject matter of his new writings. He feels himself near the wild heart of life in the changing waters, the line of seawrack, and the endless drift of seaweed. The human element he recognizes ecstatically in a girl, the embodiment of health and beauty, the purely feminine without shame or wantonness, and in his mind he welcomes her with profane joy as part of the new life. Stephen then finds shelter in a sandy nook, where he falls asleep. A new world appears to him, a world "fantastic, dim, uncertain as under sea, traversed by cloudy shapes and beings," a world he is not fully to explore until many years later in *Finnegans Wake*. He rouses, refreshed and calm, and watches the rim of the young moon embedded in the sand and the tide flowing in fast (190–201).

Chapter V.

The *theme* is the careful development and resolving of all themes in the book as the artist meets conflicting forces, both old (family, religion, politics) and new (aesthetics, science). He resolves to live abroad and write about Ireland.

The *style* is a mixture of realism and stream of consciousness, pointing toward *Ulysses*. Two long realistic episodes describing university life are separated by a highly imaginative account of the process of poetic creation. At the end is a sort of summary of all themes in diary form.

Episodes:

The artist rejects the miseries of home life, symbolized by his mother's complaints that he has given up religion by going to the university. He finds consolation in such sensual things as dripping trees after rain and in the beauty of certain books, yet the ancient words of Aristotle and Aquinas from his aesthetics classes seem dead. Even the casual words in the streets seem to be sterile; the artist must inject new meaning into them to make them come to life. Long realistic passages reproduce faithfully the conversation of university students and faculty. Stephen has learned to banter with others and to joke in pig Latin. Lengthy discussions of science and aesthetics seem to show the futility of learning (202–54).

A reverie about a girl Stephen has met contrasts with the prosaic real girl as he encounters her in other passages, showing that to the artist the mental image is more important than the deed: "In the virgin womb of the imagination the word was made flesh." The glow of mind is even keener in the darkness before the dull, white light of dawn covers the world. As his imagination glows, the poet becomes overwhelmed with desire, and the dreamer's sexual orgasm becomes linked with the pleasing, warm flow of words: "the liquid letters of speech, symbols of the element of mystery, flowed forth over his brain" (254–63).

Realistic scenes from university life are interspersed with poetic descriptions of Stephen's thoughts. Conversations with fellow-students, especially Cranly, reveal his arguments against

Irish nationalism and the Roman Catholic Church. Cranly tries to get inside Stephen's shell, but the revolt and the loneliness remain to the end. Stephen most fully characterizes himself when he tells Cranly that he will not serve what he no longer believes in, even if it means loneliness and loss of friends, and that he will try to express himself as freely and wholly as he can, using as defense the weapons of silence, exile, and cunning (263–92).

A summary of all themes is given in diary form, concisely though seemingly in no apparent order, as if the artist wished to make certain points quite clear in brief notes that resemble fragments of thought (of the catechism technique in the "Ithaca" episode of *Ulysses*, as shown on page 91 below.) Among others, the following decisions are recorded as if they were a prelude to the opening of *Ulysses*: (1) the break with his family (his mother arguing about religion, his father suggesting membership in a rowing club and the study of law); (2) the break with an unnamed girl he has been seeing; (3) the break with the Church; (4) the break with Ireland, symbolized by final resolve to be an exile; (5) the determination to be a writer, forging in the smithy of his soul the uncreated conscience of his race, symbolized by the allusion to the ancient Dedalus in the final entry: "Old father, old artificer, stand me now and ever in good stead" (292–99).

The common reader is now ready for *Ulysses*. After understanding *Dubliners* and *Portrait of the Artist. Ulysses* will not seem quite so formidable as it did. Already we know Dublin, its waterfront, its crowded streets, its bars and restaurants, its schools, and its libraries. We also know many of the people that inhabit the Dublin of *Ulysses*, some by their real names like Father Conmee, others by the same fictional names they bear in *Ulysses*. From *Dubliners*, Martin Cunningham, Lenehan, Holohan, O'Madden Burke, and Bartell D'Arcy appear again in *Ulysses*. From *Portrait of the Artist* come the associates of Stephen Dedalus—students Lynch, Cranly, Hynes, Dixon, and Temple, and Father Dolan with his pandybat. More than these, however, we know Stephen Dedalus when he was a likable schoolboy before he became the clever but rather priggish young intellectual of *Ulysses*.

Another reason we can understand *Ulysses* better now is that we have seen the gradual development of Joyce's style. The idea of the epiphany, the revealing moment in the life of a person, first exploited as separate sketches in *Dubliners*, is used in *Portrait of the Artist* for condensing the diffuse autobiography of *Stephen Hero* and crystallizing the high points in the development of the artist. In *Ulysses* it becomes the very medium for condensing the modern world into the events of one day in one city, condensing it into such compact stuff that only with careful reading is the whole story understood.

Joyce has already experimented, too, with the stream-of-consciousness technique that was to make *Ulysses* notorious and, for some, hard to read. The preceding analysis of *Portrait of the Artist* points out how Joyce shows the artist realizing the importance of the mind in portraying character. Not only does he have Stephen say that thought is more important than speech and gesture, but the most vivid passages in the book are examples of the way the young artist's imagination plays upon the events that affect him most. Nearly always this is done in the conventional

manner of older fiction by having the character described as thinking or reminiscing on past events. In a few instances, however,
Joyce jumps from action to mental picture without any transition.
For example, the term "incestuous love" in a conversation with
some of the university students leads abruptly to a paragraph describing an imagined scene of such love, the transition explained
only in a subsequent paragraph where "he frowned angrily upon
his thought."[2] And the very disjointed quality of the diary in the
final episode suggests verbless sentences that characterize random
thought in parts of *Ulysses*.

The artist has by 1914 matured from the sensitive youth,
struggling against an uncongenial environment, to the careful
writer who is not only master of his medium but also mature
enough in experience to look at people with sympathy and at
himself with detachment. Stephen Dedalus is no longer James
Joyce, for he has changed into the artistic creation of James Joyce,
ready to take his place along with other Dubliners to help fill out
the picture of modern man in his restless wanderings. The artist
Joyce has learned to create the characters of his odyssey in Dublin in an objective manner that the young Dedalus could not
have known.

Meanwhile, Joyce has tried writing in other mediums. In
1907 he published a book of short poems, *Chamber Music*. In
this period he started writing his play called *Exiles* (published in
1918). This one play and the poems Joyce wrote throughout his
life have a great interest for the biographer and the student of
Joyce's development as an artist, but the ordinary reader, suspect-

[2] Joyce, *Portrait of the Artist*, 268.

ing that Joyce did not find these mediums very congenial, will probably pass them by to spend more time on the fiction that Joyce handled better.

For a look at Joyce's use of the medium of fiction, we proceed to *Ulysses*, the misunderstood novel that introduced a new manner of writing novels.

ulysses:
OR BLOOMSDAY IN DUBLIN

The publication of *Ulysses* in 1922 marks a new era in the history of fiction. For this reason it becomes the most important and the most famous work of James Joyce. In many ways it is also the best. It is probably more talked about than read because too many barriers of misconception have been built up around it. *Ulysses* is unquestionably harder to read than *Dubliners* or *Portrait of the Artist,* but the extra effort is well repaid in the realization of the encyclopedic picture of modern life that comes from a fuller understanding of the book. In fact, in my opinion, it is hard to read largely because it is comprehensive, encyclopedic, universal—in short because Joyce has tried to pack into one book the full impact of modern life with its hope and its despair, its glory and its futility.

Ulysses *then is the third step in Joyce's picture of modern man,* and in my opinion it is also the high point of Joyce's literary career. The book was some sixteen years in gestation and nearly nine years in actual writing. We know that even when Joyce was a boy Ulysses was his favorite hero, and that in 1906 he planned a story called "Ulysses" to be added to *Dubliners,* but it "never got any forrarder than the title." Tempted to give *Dubliners* the title of "Ulysses at Dublin," he changed his mind, probably because the parallels to the old story were too remote in the series of stories to make the collection seem more than the vague odyssey of an observant writer. The genesis of *Ulysses* has been well told in Herbert Gorman's biography but even there never more concisely than in the report by one of his language students in Zurich of a conversation with Joyce in 1917: "The most beautiful, all-embracing theme is that of the *Odyssey*. It is greater, more human than that of *Hamlet, Don Quixote*, Dante, *Faust.* . . . The most beautiful, most human traits are contained in the *Odyssey*."[1]

The evolution of Joyce's attempt to express in fiction the history of modern man in terms of the regional particulars of Dublin becomes now more apparent. *Dubliners* is on the simplest level; written in plain language, it is objective even in the author's probing into the inner consciousness of the characters, and the characters and situations are so much a part of common human experience that they seem universal, at least in the broad picture of Dublin reflected in the whole collection. *Portrait of the Artist* is on a somewhat more difficult level, though still written in plain enough language to be grasped without explanation; it is nevertheless intensely subjective and by its very introspective nature reflects the innermost feelings of the main character; in style it is still mainly realistic, especially where Stephen's relations with other people dominate, but the vigorous imagination of the boy is described in terms of interior monologue that foretells the stream of consciousness in *Ulysses*.

Ulysses itself is on the third level of difficulty. It is written in a new style, or rather a variety of styles and techniques that are new and daring even though they use a vocabulary that differs

[1] Gorman, *James Joyce*, 224. The translation quoted is that of Joseph Prescott, *College English*, XV, (1954), 325.

very little from the ordinary language of realistic fiction. It is almost completely objective in its merciless picture of modern life, for the new emphasis on the inner thoughts of characters is the artist's detached way of delineating what he considers the most important thing to be known about his characters. Even the character of Stephen Dedalus, who started as the autobiographical inspiration of the whole odyssey, is described now in a detached manner, for the reader realizes more keenly now that the Stephen he follows could not be the novelist who so wisely observed life and created the Blooms and countless other Dubliners in *Ulysses*.

Finnegans Wake is on the highest level of difficulty, to put it mildly. It pursues Joyce's search of the universal to the ultimate world of dreams where names and shapes are constantly shifting, and where people, places, and events refuse to follow a realistic, or even logical, pattern. In style it is so full of novelties that the common reader has refused to have anything to do with it. Joyce here departs from the conventional English language that has served him so well, even through *Ulysses*; he creates a new vocabulary that blends many languages and countless allusions into bewildering series of linguistic fireworks that devoted critics are now engaged in explaining. The technique of this new book is so startling that it will take many years even to evaluate its artistic quality. I have tried, at the end of this study, to explain the technique and to give my critical judgment of the work. At this point it is enough to say that *Finnegans Wake* is not for the ordinary reader.

Ulysses, on the other hand, can be understood with a little help, for in it Joyce has succeeded best in combining sound and sense, making full use of stylistic novelty without obscuring his larger picture. Much of the damage done by early idolators of Joyce has been repaired by a number of recent critical studies, beginning with that of Harry Levin in 1941. But the ordinary reader still needs a simple approach to the work that will enable him to see that *Ulysses* is worth the effort of unraveling some of its difficulties. The end result will be a devastating picture of modern life, but the way to it is filled with some of the most memorable characters in all fiction as well as with much of the most masterful use of the English language since Shakespeare. *Ulysses* may be appalling, but it is good fun.

It is perhaps inevitable that a book so full of innovations as *Ulysses* should be much talked about, yet little understood. In spite of increasing numbers of readers of the book, however, a few popular misconceptions that need to be dispelled have persisted. Two of these fallacies can be disposed of quickly—that *Ulysses* is a "dirty" book, and that a complicated system of esoteric symbolism and Homeric parallels must be mastered before the work can be understood. The third fallacy—that the book belongs to the cult of unintelligibility because of a disjointed stream-of-consciousness technique—has least justification, but will take longer to refute. I should like to lead the common reader over these three hurdles and into the pleasurable reading of Joyce's masterpiece.

I can understand why the hurried reader, especially among the very young, thinks *Ulysses* is all "dirt." After all, pornography is of all knowledge the most avidly sought after and, because of its very universality, the most easily understood. Although little of *Ulysses* is devoted completely to the erotic, that little is largely concentrated in the carnal meditations of Mrs. Bloom, where they are easily got at. Joyce knew that people are much concerned with what they are too squeamish to write about, whether pertaining to sex or to bodily functions, and his artistic creed demanded that these things be described in terms that every schoolboy knows and uses rather than in the colorless euphemisms of hypocritical writing. He had already stated his case plainly as early as 1905 in his letters defending certain passages in *Dubliners* against the censorship of publishers. He had cited Chaucer as his precedent, and he might have also cited Rabelais, Dante, and Old Testament authors, too—older writers who had used the plain language of blunt men and women when it served their artistic purpose to do so.

Joyce knew that the sexual urge is one of the strongest forces in life, but the severe artist in him would not allow him to emphasize it except where the particular character concerned or the excitement of the particular episode called for such emphasis. This discrimination should be quite obvious after my analysis of *Ulysses* in the next chapter, but for the moment let us note the sane and considered verdict of Judge John M. Woolsey in 1933 when he lifted the ban on the importing of *Ulysses* into the United States. "In spite of its unusual frankness, I do not detect anywhere the leer of the sensualist. . . . The words which are criticized as dirty are old Saxon words known to almost all men and, I venture, to many women, and are such words as would be naturally and habitually used, I believe, by the types of folk whose life, physical and mental, Joyce is seeking to describe." Judge Woolsey then announces his considered opinion that *Ulysses* may be emetic but not aphrodisiac, and he backs his judgment with legal precedents and with an example of literary analysis that any critic would be proud to own.[2]

The matter of Homeric parallels is harder to answer. Joyce himself was concerned from boyhood with the idea that Ulysses was the best fictional representation of the all-round man. Even the most casual reader is willing to believe that the restless wanderer who touched all phases of life is an excellent medium for depicting the universal, but he gets a bit impatient with the prevailing fallacy that there is some sort of esoteric connection between Joyce's *Ulysses* and Homer's *Odyssey*, without a knowledge of which the reader of the modern work is lost. Joyce himself encouraged this point of view and carried every possible parallel to its farthest point. In his conversations with Stuart Gilbert he furnished enough clues literally to fill a book, one which has been very influential. Gilbert's names for the eighteen unnumbered episodes of *Ulysses* have become accepted for convenient reference in lieu of the chapter numbers Joyce omitted, but on the whole Gilbert's study of Homeric parallels has been useful only to the specialist.

Any intelligent reader, in my opinion, can read *Ulysses* and enjoy it without having read the *Odyssey*. The closest parallels can be explained by the vaguest knowledge of the ancient story as remembered from childhood reading. Careful study will add other parallels that are entertaining even if not important. But to follow with Stuart Gilbert and other Joyce cultists the mystical connections of every minor point, even though with the co-

[2] The decision is printed in the preface to the Random House edition of *Ulysses* (New York, 1934).

operation of Joyce, is to reduce the whole subject of Homeric parallels to an absurdity, obscuring the issue rather than clarifying it.

Even the most casual reader of Homer's *Odyssey* will realize that Joyce has played very freely with the older story. There is a resemblance in the main characters. Leopold Bloom is Ulysses, the restless hero, wandering physically all across Dublin and spiritually throughout the world. Molly Bloom is Penelope but in reverse, her twenty-five lovers contrasting ironically with Penelope's classic fidelity. And Stephen Dedalus is Telemachus, son of Ulysses and Penelope, yet Stephen is related to the Blooms only in Leopold's futile desire for a son.

There is also a vague resemblance to the plot of Homer's epic. Joyce opens with three episodes devoted to Stephen, even as the *Odyssey* plunges *in medias res* with Telemachus opposing his mother's suitors and going out in search of his father. (Incidentally, this opening is one of the strong points of the *Odyssey*, because it not only introduces us to Telemachus and Penelope, but also arouses an interest in what will be done to relieve the tense situation. The corresponding part in *Ulysses* is structurally weak because there is no mention of the main characters, who appear for the first time in the fourth episode. The reader is given no indication that this part of *Ulysses* is a sequel to *Portrait of the Artist*, unless he has read elsewhere about the genesis of the story.) Joyce follows with a second section containing twelve episodes of the adventures of Bloom, which parallel, very roughly to be sure, the well-known but briefly related adventures of Ulysses in Books IX–XII of the *Odyssey*. Joyce ends with a final section of three episodes depicting the homecoming of Bloom, to correspond with the entire last half of Homer's work, which comes to a magnificent climax in Ulysses' fight with the suitors to regain his wife and kingdom.

The episodes in Joyce's *Ulysses* are named for characters or themes from the *Odyssey*, mostly taken from Ulysses' adventures, that part of the *Odyssey* which is most widely known because it is a much-told tale. The lotus eating which makes Ulysses' sailors lazy and carefree fits easily into Bloom's early morning daydreams of escape from reality, including his desire to travel to the Orient. Ulysses' visit to the "Land of the Dead" in search of his companion has a ready parallel in Bloom's attending the funeral of Paddy Dignam. The windbags of Joyce's newspaper office can be recognized as kin to Aeolus, god of the winds, who ties all the winds into a bag for Ulysses; but the parallel can be properly understood only by reading Jonathan Swift's more violent attack on the windbags (Aeolists) of the eighteenth century in his *Tale of a Tub*.

Some other parallels are easy enough: the "Sirens" are the singing barmaids; Nausicaa is Gerty MacDowell, the young girl who in both stories arouses the passions of the older man; the one-eyed Cyclops is the Citizen in Kiernan's saloon, with his nationalistic prejudices and his irascible boisterousness; and Circe, who turns Ulysses' men into swine, is Bella Cohen, keeper of Dublin's brothel. But the parallels suggested by the titles of Calypso, the Lestrygonians, the Wandering Rocks, and the Oxen of the Sun, among others, are farfetched and add nothing to the enjoyment of the common reader.

Perhaps the soundest observation the critic can make, after comparing Joyce with Homer, is that Joyce usually arrives at almost the opposite effect to that of Homer's story, for the odyssey of modern man is complicated rather than direct, frustrating rather than heroic, futile in the end rather than moving. The reader, on the other hand, is inclined to forgive the many needless parallels in minor points when he thinks of *Ulysses* as adventures of modern man in conflict with his environment.

The Homeric parallels are often rewarding even though they are not necessary for the enjoyment of the common reader. To attribute to *Ulysses* additional esoteric symbolism, however, in addition to its acknowledged resemblances to the *Odyssey*, serves only to give Joyce's work an unfriendly, almost untouchable air. I refer to the elaborate scheme outlined by Stuart Gilbert, whereby each of the eighteen episodes in *Ulysses* has not only its scene, its hour of the day, and its Homeric parallels, but also is "associated with a given Organ of the human body, relates to a certain Art, has its appropriate Symbol and a specific Technic." Whether or not Joyce actually had all this elaborate paraphernalia in mind when he was writing *Ulysses* does not concern the common reader. Its very top-heaviness is absurd and often meaningless. For example, we are told that the fourth episode ("Calypso"), in which Bloom goes to the butcher shop for a kidney, returns and cooks breakfast, talks to his wife, eats, and then reads the newspaper as he sits in the privy, has for its organ the kidney, for its art economics, for its color orange, for its symbol the nymph, and for its technic mature narrative. In such episodes the connection is too remote to be of help. And in others such apparatus does not explain enough.

Misconceptions of this sort are understandable because they come usually from the general reader. Yet the belief that Joyce has nothing but a staccato and verbless style, often entirely unpunctuated, comes usually from students of literature who should know better. Joyce's style varies with his subject matter, and often shifts so fast that the reader must be versatile to follow it. But the obscurity lies in its variety and in the multiplicity of its allusions, rather than in a deliberate concealing of thought behind chaotic reminiscing.

The so-called stream-of-consciousness technique, by which thought patterns are given at least an equal place with behavior in depicting fictional characters, is not new, yet it owes its vogue and its form in the modern novel largely to the influence of *Ulysses*. The idea is at least as old as the soliloquy in drama and was consciously developed by Joyce in his earlier work, as I have already shown. The epiphany, no matter what form it may take, reveals itself as much by inner thoughts as by speech and gesture. In *Ulysses*, however, the technique became something new with the constant variation of the pattern in such a way that it led to a revolution, for better or for worse, in the technique of modern fiction. Joyce himself said that he got the idea for the "interior monologue" from an obscure French novel, Edouard Dujardin's *Les Lauriers sont Coupés*. Mrs. Mary Colum is sure that this was another of Joyce's jokes on a credulous public,[3] but the French author, we may be sure, was delighted to find his novel brought out of obscurity and reprinted. Certainly the technique was used before Joyce and before Dujardin,[4] yet it would never have been so widely used in contemporary fiction but for Joyce's genius.

[3] *Life and the Dream* (New York, Doubleday and Company, 1947), 394.
[4] The whole question is summarized by L. E. Bowling, "What is the Stream of Consciousness Technique?" *PMLA*, Vol. LXV (1950), 333–45. Joyce is the chief example used in a new critical study by Robert Humphrey, *Stream of Consciousness in the Modern Novel* (Berkeley, University of California Press, 1954).

Ulysses is not all "interior monologue." A goodly portion of the book is given over to straightforward narrative, either of a conventional sort or in the particular style chosen to fit the mood of a given episode. Whenever direct discourse is introduced it is realistic, whether it be the coarse speech of the Narrator in Kiernan's saloon ("Cyclops") or the intellectual ingenuity of Stephen's discourse on Hamlet in the library ("Scylla and Charybdis"). This would be more apparent, at least to the average American reader, if quotation marks for direct discourse were inserted by printers to replace the French punctuation with a dash adopted by Joyce.

Without the narration of conscious thought, however, *Ulysses* would be sterile and without meaning. In these passages the characters come vividly to life, revealing their past histories and their present desires. The narrative tells always of the present; the thoughts depict the past and presage the future. But the method of presenting thoughts varies considerably, becoming more complicated as the day progresses, as the active life gives way to the contemplative, and as that in turn merges into the relaxing weariness of late evening.

Let me illustrate this shifting of technique in the manner of depicting thought. The first method, quite common in the earlier episodes, and easily grasped because it has become popular in recent fiction, is the sudden but obvious shift from narrative to the inner mind of the character last described, much in the same way that the motion picture suddenly breaks the distant and panoramic view for a close-up that will reveal the facial expressions of the chief character.

In the opening episode ("Telemachus"), as Buck Mulligan

taunts him, Stephen in his thoughts relives the whole scene of his mother's death; except for this recollection all is straight narrative. In the second episode ("Nestor"), Stephen teaches his history class, and interrupts his catechism only with random thoughts on the boys; after class he talks to headmaster Deasy, and is occasionally reminded of something suggested by the conversation. For example, when Mr. Deasy mentions the financial tricks of the Jews, Stephen's thoughts break in to present a more sympathetic point of view:

> On the steps of the Paris Stock Exchange the goldskinned men quoting prices on their gemmed fingers. Gabbles of geese. They swarmed loud, uncouth about the temple, their heads thickplotting under maladroit silk hats. Not theirs: these clothes, this speech, these gestures. Their full slow eyes belied the words, the gestures eager and unoffending, but knew the rancours massed about them and knew their zeal was vain. Vain patience to heap and hoard. Time surely would scatter all. A hoard heaped by the roadside: plundered and passing on. Their eyes knew the years of wandering and, patient, knew the dishonours of their flesh.[5]

A second variation is made by complicating and extending the first. In the third episode ("Proteus"), Stephen walks along the strand of Dublin's tidal river, whose changing waters remind him of changing life, of birth and death. There is very little narrative here; the thoughts of birth are connected with two midwives he sees, and death with the recovered corpse of a drowned man. The

[5] Joyce, *Ulysses*, 35.

allusions become increasingly difficult, for the reader must have as full a mind as Stephen's to follow everything. For example, Stephen wonders what is in the midwife's bag, and hits upon the fantastic connection between the mystic's gazing upon his navel and the rigging up of a telephone line back to Adam: "A misbirth with a trailing navelcord, hushed in ruddy wool. The cords of all link back, strandentwining cable of all flesh. That is why mystic monks. Will you be as gods? Gaze in your omphalos. Hello. Kinch here. Put me on to Edenville. Aleph, alpha: nought, nought one."[6]

The difficulty of this technique used to characterize Stephen is in the rapid shifting of ideas in an active and well-stocked mind. To cite a more complicated example, Stephen is at another point reminded of Jonathan Swift's having been Dean of St. Patrick's Cathedral in Dublin in the early eighteenth century, and this reminds him of Swift's having gone mad from thinking too much upon mankind. The allusions to Swift in *cathedral, madness, Houyhnhnm,* and *dean* are unmistakable; and yet one may understand Stephen's feeling of human decay without knowing about Swift and his rational horses, the Houyhnhnms, or about the possible connection between horse faces and Stephen's friends: "The hundredheaded rabble of the cathedral close. A hater of his kind ran from them to the wood of madness, his mane foaming in the moon, his eyeballs stars. Houyhnhnm, horsenostrilled. The oval equine faces. Temple, Buck Mulligan, Foxy Campbell. Lantern jaws. Abbas father, furious dean, what offence laid fire to their brains?"[7]

With the introduction of the main character, Leopold

[6] *Ibid.,* 39.
[7] *Ibid.,* 40.

Bloom, in the fourth episode ("Calypso"), a new kind of stream of consciousness is introduced, not smooth and deeply intellectual like the tidal river of Stephen's thoughts, but swiftly flowing with constant changes like a cross-country river. In depicting the early morning thoughts of Bloom, it glides rapidly, changing at every turn by the addition of a new stream, undisturbed when flowing calmly between high banks, broken and choppy when it froths around rocks or over the falls.

Just as Stephen's flow of thoughts is difficult to follow only when he becomes intellectual and knots his everyday affairs with allusions from his wide reading, so Bloom's ordinarily lucid thoughts are made difficult by the new streams that keep coming in, most of which tie up with a recall of the past and keep recurring in bewildering combinations throughout the day. For example, when Bloom walks out to buy meat for breakfast, the prosaic figure of a middle-aged, Jewish advertisement solicitor, the reader is not disturbed by the intrusion of Major Tweedy, Bloom's father-in-law, into the romantic daydream of Oriental splendor that comes from the sight of the bright sun and the smell of fresh bread: "Makes you feel young. Somewhere in the east: early morning: set off at dawn, travel round in front of the sun, steal a day's march on him. Keep it up for ever never grow a day older technically. Walk along a strand, strange land, come to a city gate, sentry there, old ranker too, old Tweedy's moustaches leaning on a long kind of spear. Wander through awned streets. Turbaned faces going by. Dark caves of carpet shops, big man, Turko the terrible, seated crosslegged smoking a coiled pipe."[8]

On the other hand, what at first appears to be a simple event

[8] *Ibid.*, 57.

may turn out to be very important as the story develops. A good example is the introduction, during this same morning walk, of the theme words, *Agendath Netaim*. At the butcher's shop Bloom notices among the cut sheets of wrapping paper the prospectus of *Agendath Netaim*, a company that proposed to purchase sandy tracts north of Jaffa and plant them with eucalyptus, citrus fruit, olives, almonds, and melons. The idea fits beautifully into his desire to travel in Oriental lands, and so the prospectus becomes a part of his shifting mood. It is linked in his thoughts at first with restlessness and the sensuous. "Nice to hold, cool waxen fruit, hold in the hand, lift it to the nostrils and smell the perfume."[9] Then it shifts to the despair of the Jew wandering all over the earth from captivity to captivity: "A barren land, bare waste. Volcanic lake, the dead sea. No fish, weedless, sunk deep in the earth. No wind would lift those waves, grey metal, poisonous foggy waters."[10]

This is poetic language and easy to read, but, much more important to Joyce, it is also the very fiber of Bloom's character. *Agendath Netaim*, strange words, symbolize the motive described by this whole incident, and as such the words, like a recurrent theme in music, keep weaving themselves into Bloom's thoughts. During the day the motive is definitely tied with sensuousness, as when he becomes excited by looking at women's clothes in a shop window: "All for a woman, home and houses, silk webs, silver, rich fruits, spicy from Jaffa. Agendath Netaim. Wealth of the world."[11] The connection with wealth becomes dominant in the

9 *Ibid.*, 60.
10 *Ibid.*, 61.
11 *Ibid.*, 166.

evening: in imagination he has bought extensively and then lost his investment by heavy mortgages.[12] One of his last acts after midnight is to take the folded circular out of his pocket and burn it,[13] adding *Agendath* to his other abortive schemes for making money.[14]

This method of symbolizing traits of character by means of words or phrases that recall whole incidents has been compared to the use of musical leitmotivs in a Wagner opera. The artistic purpose is similar, but Joyce's use of the themes is far more complicated than Wagner's, because of their greater number and because of the economical method of using a single word or phrase to recall scenes from the past. The reader has to be constantly on the alert not to miss the first declaration of the full theme or the association key words that recall it in its later entrances. This requires a mental agility that is repaid not only in the fuller understanding of Joyce's artistic purpose, but also—perhaps a baser pleasure—in the satisfaction of solving the mystery by keeping the important clues always in mind.

The themes are associated with individuals, most of them with Stephen Dedalus and Leopold Bloom. The common reader will find Stephen's themes intellectual and hard to follow, and perhaps he will find them not too rewarding, beyond showing the brilliant versatility of a young man who is spiritually lost. The themes connected with Bloom and his family, however, are earthy and practical; they seem to be merely the casual echoes of everyday incidents, but they become the essence of tragedy.

For example, the important themes of *Ulysses* associated with Bloom are those of his family life: the beautiful days of his

12 *Ibid.*, 456.   13 *Ibid.*, 691.   14 *Ibid.*, 703.

early married life with Molly; the infidelities of Molly tied up at the time of the story with Blazes Boylan ("jingle jaunty jingle") and with snatches of an old song ("Your head it simply swirls, Those lovely seaside girls"); the daughter Milly who is becoming like her mother; and the two tragedies of his life, the death of his only son Rudy as an infant and the suicide of his father. Countless minor themes swirl in and out of his thoughts: the business of advertising that is his livelihood; the prize titbit of a story he is going to write; the sticky lemon soap that keeps bothering him all day; the *Sweets of Sin* he bought for his wife to read; the secret correspondence he has kept up with Martha Clifford under the name of Henry Flower; the four o'clock appointment of Boylan and Molly.[15] But these and many other verbal themes weave themselves gradually into the larger pattern of Bloom's desire for fatherhood, which ends in a compromise between restlessness on the one hand and tolerant resignation on the other. They all resolve themselves at last in Bloom's solicitous adoption of Stephen, drunk and helpless in a brothel, as his vicarious son.

With a good deal of alertness and some practice, any intelligent reader can understand *Ulysses* enough to enjoy the tragedy of the characters and the comedy of the incidental satire, the versatile handling of the language and the distilled picture of modern life. There are, of course, other things to bother even the eager reader than those I have analyzed. Some of these, such as the special techniques in which Joyce appears to be more interested in

[15] An index of verbal motifs associated with Bloom and Stephen has been compiled by Richard M. Kain, *Fabulous Voyager* (Chicago, University of Chicago Press, 1947), App. D. 277–89. Other verbal associations may be easily followed with the help of Miles L. Hanley's *Word Index to James Joyce's Ulysses* (Madison, Wisconsin, 1937).

showing his virtuosity than in telling his story, I have attempted to explain in the next two chapters.

Another source of difficulty in reading *Ulysses* is what I call "sympathetic arrogance of Irishmen toward things Irish." Joyce seems to have been cursed with the gift of total recall, and the resulting picture of Irish culture is so Celtic that Irish critics think that only they can understand him. Perhaps we understand all we need, for when Joyce properly disciplines his memory we can see Dublin in the early twentieth century as vividly as we see Chaucer's medieval London from the *Canterbury Tales*. In its less inspired moments, however, Joyce's gift of memory annoys us with trivia that we cannot understand because we did not happen to live in Dublin in 1904. For example, we can reconstruct popular songs and understand Dublin slang only from the context, whereas the references to the hermetic cult of the Irish poet AE (George William Russell) and the interest of the group in Hindu mysticism are frequent and full enough to allow us to reconstruct the movement or at least Joyce's scorn of it.

We must remember that Joyce is only doing in a more compact fashion what other artists have done—describing the *mundus alter et idem* that excites our curiosity by the novelty of the world different from our own and at the same time suspends our disbelief by the nostalgia of a world familiar to us. The only fly in the ointment is that Irish critics keep reminding us in a patronizing way that we cannot possibly understand Joyce because we are not Irishmen of their generation. Joyce with his infinite detail has made this "other world" live for us, and we know it much better than we would have known it without him. If we cannot understand these things Irish after a careful and sympathetic reading, perhaps it means that they do not belong in a great book. After all, our understanding of things Irish may prove to be a good test of what is ephemeral.

Into the eighteen episodes of *Ulysses* Joyce has poured infinite detail with a lavish variety of style. The Blooms and Stephen Dedalus have hidden nothing from us, and the two hundred or so other characters have added multiple variations of life to make up the total picture of modern man in a scientific civilization. There is little nobility in it, but there is a vast amount of mingled tenderness and brutality, laughter and tears.

To those who say that we might have been spared some of the sordid details, we can only say that this was not Joyce's way. He selected his material more rigidly than most artists, for even where he approaches most nearly the psychoanalytic method of uninhibited reverie, he chooses only those details that show the complete picture. In the "Penelope" episode, for example, Joyce depicts Molly Bloom, not only in her reminiscence of sexual adventures but also in her casual thoughts of dress and travel, and the homely trivialities of everyday household affairs. He pictures Molly's earthiness as much in her innate disdain for the intellectual as in her erotic thoughts. Again, in the "Circe" episode, that Freudian orgy in a brothel, the most intimate, and sometimes disgusting, passages are carefully selected to show the bisexual, compromising, tolerant, often lovable nature of Leopold Bloom.

With all its faults, *Ulysses* is one of the great books of modern literature. The full picture it gives of our complicated civilization, whether we like that picture or not, makes the book worth reading, and the technical experiments make the picture seem always fresh. Joyce peels the husks off old words and makes them glow with new meaning. He is always striving to enlarge his medium, and the innovations make for hard reading. But he has not yet abandoned his conventional medium—we must wait for *Finnegans Wake* for that. With some industry and a little help, *Ulysses* can be understood by the common reader, and it is fun to try.

CHAPTER FIVE

AN ANALYSIS OF ulysses

Ulysses, as we can now see, is the odyssey of modern man wandering restlessly in search of a possible answer to the problem of his relation to the seeming futility of modern civilization. Leopold Bloom, half-Jewish citizen of Ireland, lives out his own past and the history of Everyman in the ordinary events of one day, June 16, 1904, in the one city of Dublin.

The book begins as a sequel to *Portrait of the Artist*, which is the way Joyce first planned it. The first three episodes belong to Stephen Dedalus, that brilliant but frustrated young intellectual whose early life was the subject of *Portrait of the Artist*. And the last episode belongs to Molly, Bloom's wife, whose uninhibited thoughts at the end of the day let the eternal feminine have the last word. But the main story is Bloom's, certainly after he is introduced in the fourth episode, even in those scenes where he only hovers on the fringes of the main action, as in the library or at the maternity hospital.

Roughly, *Ulysses* is divided into three parts, distinctly indicated typographically by Roman numerals and, in the American edition, by huge initial letters that cover a whole page each. (The eighteen episodes or chapters have no numbers or titles printed in the original book or in reprints.) The first part (episodes 1–3) is given wholly to Stephen's morning activities, the second part (episodes 4–15) to the adventures during the day of Bloom and Stephen and many other Dubliners, and the third part (episodes 16–18) to the homecoming of Bloom and Stephen after midnight.

Artistically, the plan of the book is much more complicated, though the author gives the reader no other hint except to point out by his title, *Ulysses*, that some sort of parallel to the Greek epic of Homer is to be expected. The common reader is somewhat baffled by the intellectual atmosphere of the first part, unless he has been prepared for it by reading *Portrait of the Artist*. By the time he gets into the puzzling intricacies of the third episode he is ready to give up (and too frequently he does give up at this very point). It is not until later, if he gets that far, that he sees Stephen as a necessary counterpart to Bloom's practical earthiness. He may never see that the three episodes of Stephen (1–3) exactly parallel the first three of Bloom (4–6), not only in time of day (roughly, eight, ten, and eleven o'clock in the morning), but also in general theme.

The parallel of themes in these two sections needs more explanation.[1] The first episodes in each pair (1,4) contain the obvious correspondence of the breakfast scenes and the clarity of early morning, but the contrast between the natures of the two men may be clearly seen in their reactions to the events and bits of conversation that go on around them. Stephen's introspective

[1] S. Foster Damon, in a footnote to his essay, "The Odyssey in Dublin," *James Joyce: Two Decades of Criticism*, 211, calls attention to this parallel as a part of the way the book is built in groups of threes, and cites Ezra Pound's earlier analogy (*Mercure de France*, June 1, 1922) of *Ulysses* with the musical structure of the sonata, where Stephen's problems constitute the first theme, Bloom's the second, then both are developed and extended at length, and finally united in the recapitulation of Part III.

nature makes him brood over his seeming guilt in the death of his mother and over his desire to search for a spiritual father to replace the uncongenial Simon Dedalus. On the other hand, Bloom's earthy nature is shown by his reactions to his wife and his daughter and to the natural bodily functions of early morning, while his sensitive inner thoughts find expression in the mingled elation and despair aroused by contemplation of a Palestine homeland for his wandering race. Of the two characters, Bloom's is the more complete, the more natural, and the more apt to arouse the interest of the reader opening the book for the first time. In other words, for the common reader *Ulysses* should begin with Part II.

After announcing the contrasting themes in the first episodes (1,4), Joyce uses the second episodes of each pair (2,5) to develop the ideas by showing the futility of escape from the humiliation and frustration of everyday existence. Stephen learns that history, the intellectual escape into the past, is futile and even boring when handled by schoolboys. More elaborately, Bloom rejects, one after the other, the geographical escape by travel, the amatory escape of an illicit love affair, and the religious escape of the Church, but accepts the physical luxury of a warm bath.

The third episodes in each pair (3,6) deal with the profound idea of change reiterated in the age-old sequence of birth, life, death, and rebirth, the cycle that Joyce borrows from the eighteenth-century philosophy of Vico and later uses as his main theme in *Finnegans Wake*.

With Stephen the idea of change is suggested by the changing tide and by what he sees along the beach, but the complexity of the episode comes from Stephen's own skeptical nature and his introspective fondness for mystical philosophy. With Bloom, on the other hand, the idea of change comes from thinking on death as he follows the corpse of his friend Dignam to the cemetery, for death is tied in his mind with the beautiful early love of Molly that preceded the birth of his son, who died in infancy. Stephen's episode is packed with philosophy and learning, Bloom's with the seething life of Dublin and with popular, even humorous, ideas about death. Stephen's episode is intellectual and at first intimidating; Bloom's is racy and easy to read. For the common reader, it is unfortunate that the two are not reversed in order.

The long development that follows, in the last nine episodes of Part II, extends the themes that have been announced in the first six episodes. During the busy noon hours the hurried bustle of the city swirls around Stephen, Leopold, and the many other Dubliners who pass by engaged in their casual everyday routine. First there is the confusion of a city newspaper office, just as the racing special comes off the press and the editorial staff gets ready to go out for lunch. Bloom is there to arrange for an advertisement, and Stephen to deliver a letter to the editor, but they do not meet. Then comes the busy lunch hour, when Bloom resumes his lonely wanderings across Dublin; the seething activity of life reaches a climax with mass mastication at Burton's, but the episode belongs to Bloom, traveling alone and meditating as he goes.

A quiet interlude follows at the library, where Stephen is the center of attention as he explains, with sparkling brilliance, his theory of Hamlet. The episode is deeply intellectual, but the style is vastly amusing to those who can follow the mental dexterity of Stephen's arguments. After this comes the episode where Dublin parades before our eyes in a number of short scenes tied together by the varying ways the many Dubliners greet the procession across the city of the viceroy, symbol of England's dominance over Ireland. Stephen and Bloom are seen, each for a moment, submerged in the complexity and bustle of the city in its mid-afternoon activity.

The next three episodes (11–13) are Bloom's, except where the author is carried away by his cleverness in the special techniques he employs. First, Bloom sits in the Ormond bar and listens to the music and joking, which accentuates his loneliness. Next, he goes to Kiernan's saloon to meet Martin Cunningham about Paddy Dignam's insurance. Waiting for Cunningham, Bloom falls into talk with several garrulous barflies whose tongues get looser as the drinks flow more freely. The two who talk most remain without names, the Narrator and the ultrapatriotic Citizen. Bloom talks more than before, but his attempts to answer the half-drunken prejudices of the barflies merely antagonize them the more. At the end he barely escapes without violence. The third of these three scenes of Bloom's is a quiet twilight hour on Sandymount Beach, and for the first half of the episode Bloom is not identified. In the language of a sentimental novel the longings of a young girl are displayed, inspired by a middle-aged man who watches her close by. The reader realizes that the man is Bloom, who becomes so excited by his thoughts and the sight of the girl's underclothes that his passion reaches a climax—simultaneously with the burst of a rocket in the air. The rest of the episode is Bloom's reliving of the past in the spirit of the weariness that follows ecstasy.

In the last two episodes of Part II (14–15) Bloom and Stephen finally come together. The first meeting is at the maternity hospital where Bloom has gone to inquire about Mrs. Purefoy and joins a rollicking group of carousing young men that includes Stephen and his friends. Later they appear together in the brothel of Bella Cohen where Bloom solicitously protects Stephen, who has by this time become somewhat intoxicated.

This self-appointed role of protector is continued into Part III without break. Stephen and Bloom go out together to a cabman's shelter, Bloom solicitous and anxious to impress Stephen with his sympathy, Stephen somewhat dazed from the hangover and the weariness of one o'clock in the morning. It is two o'clock when they finally reach Bloom's kitchen, where in factual, question-and-answer style all the riddles of the book are solved as the two drink cocoa together. The final answer, if there can be an answer, is given in the last episode, where Molly lies in bed thinking of what Bloom has just told her and of her past experiences. The book ends in a lyrical acceptance of life—a whole-bodied, feminine affirmation—that seems to complete the circle, soon to bring us to another day.

This brief analysis of a complicated book reveals the carefully studied artistic plan of the author, and the reader must keep this plan in mind when he is tempted at times to be carried away by the ingenuity of individual episodes. Of course, these brilliant passages must be marked and saved for more leisurely study: the sparkling word play of Stephen and his companions, in sober setting in the newspaper office but convivial at the maternity hospital; the comic satire, gentle and playful as we listen to the afternoon music in the Ormond Hotel, rough and boisterous as Bloom and the men in Kiernan's saloon argue in the late afternoon; the coldly brilliant conversations in the library contrasted with the studied dullness of the walk from the brothel to Bloom's house in the weary hours after midnight. These are the marks of the ingenious craftsman that keep some of us going back to *Ulysses* after the first reading. But the common reader, in his first reading, must keep in mind the main purpose, and these other things will be added to his later pleasure. For this reason, let us take as a guide a brief analysis of each episode as it comes in the book, giving first the name from the Homeric parallel by which the episode is now commonly known, then the place and time of day, and then what seems necessary for the common reader to know in order to read the episode intelligently.

> *Stephen's morning adventures,*
> *sometimes called the Telemachiad.*

1. "Telemachus." 8:00 A.M. Martello Tower overlooking Dublin Bay.[2] The episode describes, mainly in simple narrative style, Stephen and his roommate, Malachi ("Buck") Mulligan, shaving and eating breakfast in the tower by the sea, and afterwards going down by the water. A young Englishman, Haines, has been invited by Mulligan to share the quarters paid for by Stephen. The natural antipathy of Stephen to Mulligan is intensified by the appearance of this "usurper," and at the end Stephen determines not to come back. The whole scene is taken up with the taunts of Mulligan, brash young medical student, pagan extrovert, who tortures Stephen by reminding him that he refused to

[2] Photographs of Martello Tower and of the bay as seen from the tower are reproduced in Patricia Hutchins, *James Joyce's Dublin* (London, Grey Walls Press, 1950).

pray at his mother's deathbed and thus rejected his mother and the Church at the same time. This is symbolized in two phrases that will haunt Stephen during the day: *heresiarch* to remind him of heresy against the Church, and *agenbite of inwit*, the medieval English poem whose title so vividly translates his own guilty "prick of conscience." There are some casual reminders of the parallel with Bloom's first episode.[3] The cloud that comes across the sun shadows "the bay in deeper green" and reminds Stephen poignantly of the bowl of "green sluggish bile" that symbolizes his mother's death: "Her door was open: she wanted to hear my music. Silent with awe and pity I went to her bedside. She was crying in her wretched bed."[4] The same cloud changes Bloom's elated reverie on the Oriental splendor of a new Jewish homeland to the gray desolation of Sodom and Gomorrah and "the oldest people" wandering from captivity to captivity, merging with Bloom's own feeling of "age crusting him with a salt cloak."[5] The comic pantomime of Turko the terrible, which Stephen associates with his mother[6] turns up again in Bloom's first Oriental reverie.[7] Finally, the sweet young thing, the "photo girl" whom Mulligan's brother knows at Westmeath,[8] is identified as Bloom's daughter Milly in a letter from her to her father.[9]

2. "Nestor." About 9:45 A.M. Deasy's school for boys. This episode is short and factual, in striking contrast to the one that follows. It opens with Stephen's monotonous questioning of the boys in his history class, but Stephen's thoughts are on the philosophy of history: time has branded these stories from the past "and fettered they are lodged in the room of the infinite possi-

---

[3] Joyce, *Ulysses*, 4.   [5] *Ibid.*, 61.   [7] *Ibid.*, 57.   [9] *Ibid.*, 66.
[4] *Ibid.*, 11.   [6] *Ibid.*, 11.   [8] *Ibid.*, 23.

bilities they have ousted." The class goes on to Milton's "Lycidas," but again Stephen is reminded of the past and the way he and other readers in the library at Paris fed like parasites upon the past: "Fed and feeding brains about me: under glowlamps, impaled, with faintly beating feelers: and in my mind's darkness a sloth of the underworld, reluctant, shy of brightness, shifting her dragon scaly folds."[10] The boys rush out to play hockey at ten o'clock, and Stephen lingers to help a backward student, thinking how this unattractive snail would have been squashed except for a mother's love.

Mr. Deasy, the headmaster, comes in to pay Stephen, reminding him how important money is to respectability. Mr. Deasy is the solid, respectable, dull citizen, who blames England's troubles on the financial tricks of the Jews and takes tremendous pride in a letter he has composed for the newspaper on the foot-and-mouth disease. Stephen in his mind resents all that Deasy stands for, though he takes the letter and agrees to give it to an editor he knows.

3. "Proteus." 11:00 A.M. Sandymount Beach. Stephen walks along the beach before going to the newspaper office to deliver Deasy's article, and his mind is whirling with the thoughts aroused by his morning activities and by the imminent change that must soon take place to solve his quandary. In Homer's story, Proteus is the creature that constantly changed shape to escape telling Menelaus what he wanted to know; thus Proteus becomes here the fitting symbol of Stephen's rapidly shifting thoughts as well as of the fundamental idea of change that makes up life itself, the ever recurring cycle of birth, life, death, and resurrection or re-

10 *Ibid.*, 26.

birth. Very little action takes place: Stephen walks across the beach, crunching the shells and listening to the waves splash and watching the tidal change in the waters, while in the distance he occasionally notices other creatures on the beach. Two midwives pass, a man and woman walk by while their dog runs up and down the beach, the bloated carcass of a dead dog ties in with the expected recovery of the corpse of a man drowned nine days before, and at the end a three-master sails into harbor.

The bulk of the episode, however, is given to Stephen's changing thoughts. Part of this flux is taken up with philosophical reflection: birth symbolizing the strands of life going back through the past to the Garden of Eden; death and gruesome bodily decay; shells and other relics of time; the vain attempt to catch the fleeting moments in words that change even as the waters. His search for words ties in with the desire for the immortality that comes from writing, from sending your epiphanies "to all the great libraries of the world, including Alexandria," only to have them fade into forgetful futility: "When one reads these strange pages of one long gone one feels that one is at one with one who once . . ."[11]

Such is the thought that comes through Stephen's eyes, that "ineluctable modality of the visible" which makes the episode perplexing to the common reader though deeply rewarding on second reading. Even as he reads these "signatures of all things" in the seaspawn and the tide, Stephen also relives the changes in his own life: his student days in Paris; his rejection of the priesthood and with it the Church; his intense interest in words and his desire to express himself in writing or in conversation; his wish to

[11] *Ibid.*, 41.

be like the bold Irish heroes of his native land mingled with the realization that he fears death so strongly that he would not dive to save a drowning man; and his darkly expressed love life tied in with passive homosexuality. At the end he has made his decision: Mulligan may keep the key to their tower, for he will not go back there. He is now homeless, for his mother is dead and his extrovert father is spiritually dead to him. While difficult to understand because of its mystical philosophy and deep intellectuality, this episode nevertheless assumes importance when we realize that this day is momentous for Stephen as he searches for something to call home, which will become the symbol of his affection.

Leopold Bloom's adventures
from breakfast until midnight.

4. "Calypso." 8:00 A.M. Bloom's house (7 Eccles Street) and the surrounding neighborhood. In this episode the main character is first introduced, but by the end of the chapter the reader feels that he knows this modern Ulysses well. Bloom is so much like all of us that we understand him, whether in the commonplace events of getting up, cooking breakfast, talking to his wife, and taking care of his bodily needs, or in his secret longings to travel into faraway lands, to love all women and yet have a home and a son to carry on his name, to have pride in his ancient Jewish heritage and yet be a loyal Irishman, to dream of wealth and luxury and yet be able to appreciate the simple delights of fresh-baked bread or a kidney sizzling in the pan. This multiplicity of common everyday details makes it very easy for the critic to use this episode to explain the author's method of depicting character.

In this episode, Bloom's thoughts merge into his everyday activities and enrich what would otherwise be a dull picture of a prosaic man in an endless round of futile adventures. The many-sided picture is so rich that the reader has to pause a good while before he realizes why the episode is called "Calypso" in honor of the nymph who took such good care of Ulysses as to make him forget for a while that he was stranded on her island far from home. To be sure, the nymph is at Bloom's house, symbolically in the picture over his bed, and actually in the thoughts of his idyllic early life with the luscious nymph Molly. It is true that Molly is the reverse of Homer's Calypso as she lies abed waiting for Leopold to bring her breakfast while she plots the current infidelity with her concert manager, Blazes Boylan, when they meet that afternoon to plan their next tour. Bloom knows all this and accepts it with tolerance, reminded that the cycle is about to begin again when he reads a letter from his daughter Milly, who is becoming like her mother in every way.

In addition to introducing the Bloom family, this episode casually brings in several smaller themes that do not assume importance until later episodes. As he goes out to the butcher's, Bloom peeps inside the leather band of his hat to see the white slip of paper, which he later hands to the clerk at the post office in order to claim a letter written by a passionate secret correspondent, Martha Clifford, whom he has not yet seen. At the same time he feels in his pocket the potato, his good-luck piece, that appears frequently later in the day. Molly asks him the meaning of the word "metempsychosis," which she found in her book, and he explains it as a sort of reincarnation. Molly forgets about it except for the ludicrous mispronunciation of it as "met him pike hoses," but to Bloom the word symbolizes the rebirth that completes the Viconian cycle and also suggests the transmigration of souls from animals to man. Add to this the fully developed theme of *Agendath Netaim*, already explained, plus the longing of Bloom for a son, merely mentioned here as Milly's frivolity reminds him of the death of his only son Rudy, and the reader will see the importance of this episode to the book as a whole while he relishes its narrative zest.

5. "The Lotus-Eaters." About 9:45 A.M. Bloom walks from his house in northwest Dublin to the southeastern section, by way of the quay, Westland Row, Trinity College, to the baths on Tara Street.

This episode describes Bloom's aimless wanderings while waiting for Dignam's funeral. He enjoys the contemplation of various ways of escape from the responsibilities of the everyday world. He looks in a tea window and dreams of travel into an Oriental world where it is sweet to do nothing.[12] He stops at the post office for a letter from Martha Clifford and revels in the thoughts of a love affair with his secret correspondent whom he has not yet seen.[13] He passes some time watching a Communion service in a church and considers religious escape.[14] Finally he seeks physical enjoyment from the perfume of a lotion he orders for Molly and from contemplation of a warm bath with a lemon-scented soap.[15]

Like the episodes just before and just after, this chapter is still simple in style, full of narrative and conversation that blend with Bloom's not too complicated thoughts. This is the dreamy,

[12] *Ibid.*, 70.
[13] *Ibid.*, 77.
[14] *Ibid.*, 79.
[15] *Ibid.*, 85.

romantic Bloom, sensuous lover of luxury, who is ready to enjoy the lotus-eating mood before he faces the reality of death at Dignam's funeral to remind him of the tragedies that death has brought into his own life. Very little realistic narrative intrudes except that concerning the life of the city. He meets C. P. McCoy as he leaves the post office and chats for a moment, though he is more interested in watching the silk-stockinged legs of a woman getting into a vehicle. Later he meets Bantam Lyons, who takes a chance remark of Bloom's for a tip on the dark horse that later in the day wins the Ascot Gold Cup. Lyons hurries away to place his bet, but the supposed tip causes Bloom much trouble later.

6. "Hades." 11:00 A.M. Funeral procession across the city, northwest to cemetery. The episode realistically describes the city itself, the conversation of the men in the carriage, and the burial of Paddy Dignam. Interspersed with the description of a cross-section of a busy city and the racy gossip of his companions, Bloom's own thoughts now become more complicated. The dominant themes are the deaths of his son and his father, both keen and untimely losses. Yet before he leaves the cemetery, we have contemplated with Bloom almost every phase of death: the slaughter of animals; the burial of customs of various nations; the idea of immortality with the grotesque picture of what a resurrection would be; the horror of being buried alive and the joke of having a gramophone in every grave; the decomposition of the body and the vanity of human wishes typified by "an obese gray rat" that keeps coming back into his thoughts later in the day; and many others. Out of death comes new life in a never ending cycle, as out of decaying flesh comes fertility for the earth. Grim Irish jokes about death contrast with sentimental death notices, and the

burial service of the Church with necrophilia. Almost nothing is left out, and yet all is introduced naturally. The whole "Hades" episode, in fact, is one of the finest examples of thematic development in the entire book.

In addition to the magnificent display of all aspects of the theme of death, this episode also brings out more sharply some parts of the main story. The suicide of Bloom's father is described for the first time. Molly's sensuous nature is accentuated, not only by Bloom's poignant memories of their early sexual adventures but also by the casual remarks of other men in the funeral carriage, leering and lascivious. Stephen's father, Simon Dedalus, is seen in the flesh, and from his remarks about Stephen and Mulligan we get a firsthand picture of the blunt extrovert that contrasts so strikingly with his son. Most important of all, we see more deeply into the nature of Bloom himself, tolerant and resigned to the insults, spoken and implied, of his companions, but at the same time poignantly aware of the sympathy of Martin Cunningham, the stupid smugness of John Henry Menton, and the "noisy selfwilled" manner of Simon Dedalus. Bloom joins casually in the conversation in the carriage, but in his mind we see his real feelings about the men with him, about his family, about his desires, about death and man's futile efforts to overcome his fear of death.

7. "Aeolus." Noon. Editorial rooms of the *Freeman's Journal* in the center of Dublin. In this bustling scene of clanging presses and jocular conversations of newspapermen, the physical activity of Dublin reaches its peak. Here we get a glimpse of Bloom at his business of soliciting advertisements, as he comes to arrange a special "plug" for one of his clients. Here Stephen comes,

too, to deliver Deasy's letter to the editor, but Bloom is too busy to do more than notice him in passing. Stephen seems at home in the witty company of the press but passes over in silence the editor's request to write for the paper himself.

In this episode Joyce for the first time departs from the depicting of character to the portrayal of modern life by means of a special technique. The style is conventional enough, even realistic in the sense that Lenehan is the sort of jokester who constantly plays on words, and that the other journalists are merely portraying their professional gifts of memory and profuse language. The reader is alerted, however, to the satire on wordiness by the typographical device of punctuating the narrative with satirical phrases made to resemble newspaper headlines. The devices of rhetoric are paraded by the gentlemen of the press, all the way from pure bombast made of endless clichés to polished oratory of balanced precision. This is a parody of modern journalese that is not so conscious as the later orgy of words in Kiernan's saloon (episode 12), but the purpose is similar, to puncture the bubble of verbiage and to depict the modern Aeolists (windbags) as vigorously as Swift disposed of the bombastic ranters of the eighteenth century in A *Tale of a Tub*. The comedy of the episode is carried along in a constant atmosphere of good-humored joking, and the headlines become racier and slangier until they reach a peak in "Sophist Wallops Haughty Helen Square on Proboscis. Spartans Gnash Molars. Ithacans Vow Pen Is Champ."[16] The common reader will find the episode easy to read and very good fun. It is a fine introduction to Joyce in his most original role, that of the comic satirist.

[16] *Ibid.*, 147.

8. "The Lestrygonians." 1:00 P.M. Bloom's tour across Dublin from the river by way of Grafton Street south to the museum. Around the wanderer is the vast ebb and flow of crowded city life, while in his mind flow his individual rememberings and desires: "Things go on same; day after day: squads of police marching out, back: trams in, out. Those two loonies mooching about. Dignam carted off. Mina Purefoy swollen belly on a bed groaning to have a child tugged out of her . . . Cityful passing away, other cityful coming, passing away too: others coming on, passing on."[17] Through this flux of life Bloom's personal thoughts are woven: his business of advertising; the horrors of mass eating at the Burton restaurant from which he retreats; the quieter atmosphere of Davy Byrne's pub where he lunches on a sandwich and a glass of burgundy while he exchanges trivialities of conversation with casual acquaintances. "Glowing wine on his palate lingered swallowed" revives memories of a youthful scene of passionate love when he proposed to Molly on Howth Hill.[18]

The parallel with Homer's Lestrygonian cannibals and their obsession with hunger is easy to see in the city at lunchtime, but this is actually only one small part of the episode. The real theme is Bloom's loneliness in the very middle of the busy life of a city. Again and again he is reminded of the beautiful days of his early married life: "Happy, happier then." The city flows around him, occasionally touching him, as when Mrs. Breen stops to tell about her husband and chat about poor Mina Purefoy in the pains of childbirth. For a moment he almost changes his mind: "I was happier then. Or was that I? Or am I now I? Twenty-eight I was. She was twenty-three when we left Lombard Street west some-

[17] Ibid., 162.   [18] Ibid., 173.

thing changed. Could never like it again after Rudy. Can't bring back time. Like holding water in your hand."[19] Then Bloom sees the luxurious women's clothes in the shops of Grafton Street, and his mind comes back to craving for love: "Perfume of embraces all him assailed. With hungered flesh obscurely, he mutely craved to adore."[20] Next follow the two contrasting pictures of eating, the mass cannibalism of Burton's and the quieter lunch on a cheese sandwich and burgundy at Davy Byrne's. The wine glowing in his blood sends him back again to a voluptuous scene with Molly, even while the talk of Davy Byrne and Nosey Flynn remind him that things are not so now. The episode ends as Bloom, having reached the museum on Kildare Street, ducks into the building to escape meeting Molly's present lover with his straw hat, tan shoes, and turned-up trousers. Bloom knows he is defeated but wishes to delude himself and escape admitting it.

9. "Scylla and Charybdis." 2:00 P.M. National Library. In the narrative of Bloom and the city which is his world, this episode is a quiet interlude, dominated by literary talk and the brilliant intellectuality of Stephen. To the common reader, it is as difficult to read as that other scene of Stephen's where he walks along the beach, but this time the interest is not kept up by the fresh air of the seashore and the perennially important idea of change. The whole episode adds little to the story: Bloom is there consulting a provincial newspaper but he remains obsequiously on the fringes; Stephen dominates the scene with his brilliant but futile literary arguments.

As the newspaper episode is a satire on wordiness in all forms,

[19] *Ibid.*, 165.
[20] *Ibid.*, 166.

so the scene in the library, where Stephen proclaims his ingenious theory concerning Hamlet to Dublin's intellectuals, portrays the futility of the literary criticism that is brilliant on the surface but lacking in fundamental ideas. Here Stephen, at his best, argues that Hamlet is the spirit of Shakespeare's dead son Hamnet and that the poet is one with the ghost of the King, the part he played in the theater; and yet at the end Stephen confesses that he does not believe the theory he has so elaborately built up.

The style of this episode gleams with allusions to the contemporary writers of the Celtic renaissance as well as to earlier literature, to Dante, to the Church Fathers, and especially to the Elizabethan background of the main argument going on between Stephen and his companions concerning Shakespeare. An analysis of a single speech of Stephen's on Shakespeare will illustrate the use of literary allusions. "He had a good groatsworth of wit and no truant memory."[21] says Stephen of Shakespeare, paraphrasing the pamphlet of Robert Green (about 1592) that contains one of the first contemporary references to the young playwright in London. In the paragraph that follows, Shakespeare's youthful poem, *Venus and Adonis* is not only mentioned by name but also is taken as symbolic of Stephen's argument that the older woman, Ann Hathaway, seduced the boy Shakespeare even as Venus bent over the boy Adonis "as prologue to the swelling act." Scenes and phrases are used from the poem but woven together to give a pleasing recollection of brilliant Elizabethan talk. The vivid hunting scene in Shakespeare's poem comes alive in Stephen's analogy of the trembling hare trying to outwit the hounds: "Poor Wat, sitting in his form, the cry of hounds, the studded bridle and

[21] *Ibid.*, 188.

her blue windows." For good measure, Stephen refers to two plays of Shakespeare as well as to *The Passionate Pilgrim* (1599), a collection of poetry attributed to him. To top off the Elizabethan flavor of the passage, Stephen produces a pun that Shakespeare would have been proud to own: "If others have their will Ann hath a way."

10. "The Wandering Rocks." 3:00 P.M. Eighteen scenes in at least fifteen different parts of Dublin, covering the entire central part of the city, ending with a nineteenth scene that serves to join the others together. This episode depicts objectively, in condensed epiphanies like those of *Dubliners*, the stream of life in a cross-section of Dublin. In the eighteen scenes some fifty characters pass by, each of them intent upon his own business but all related in some way to Bloom's story, for they are the companions of the modern man's odyssey. To tie the scenes together, the splendid procession of the English Viceroy is seen at the end of the episode driving across the city, greeted in various ways by the Irish citizens. The whole episode is a slice of life done in counterpoint, an intensification of the little stories that blend with the larger story of Bloom. Incidentally, it is probably the best of many satirical comments on Irish politics in *Ulysses*.

11. "The Sirens." 4:00 P.M. The bar and adjoining rooms at the Ormond Hotel. In this episode, Joyce, himself an accomplished musician, uses music as his subject and in style attempts to adapt some of the techniques of music to writing. The story is almost forgotten except to emphasize the loneliness of Bloom as he sits in a room adjoining the Ormond bar and composes an answer to the letter of his secret correspondent, Martha Clifford. Even as he sits there, Blazes Boylan comes to the bar, jokes with

Lenehan for a moment, and then jauntily goes to his afternoon appointment with Mrs. Bloom.

The reader is aware of the musical background from start to finish, but the technique is not at all clear. Stated very simply, a number of announced themes play hide-and-seek in the manner of a fugue while Bloom listens to a few Dublin barflies joke with the barmaids and sing some of their favorite songs. Joyce says he is here using the technique of the *fuga per canonem*, which is the simplest form of musical fugue in that it declares the theme and then repeats the notes in exact sequence but at a specified interval higher or lower—say in octaves, fifths, or tenths. The technique, in my opinion, loses the desired effect because the declaration of themes at the beginning, which should be very clear, is made incomprehensible by a succession of fragmentary phrases obviously picked out from the fugue development and later inserted at the beginning as a sort of overture. The development is clear enough, and from this portion of the episode we see a few outstanding ideas that might be called themes: "bronze by gold," the two barmaids; "jingle jingle jaunted jingling." Boylan who comes here just before his appointment with Mrs. Bloom; "I feel so sad. P.S. So lonely blooming," Bloom composing his letter to Martha even as he acquiesces in his wife's infidelity; and the crescendo of "Tap. Tap." as the distant cane of the blind stripling approaches.

Yet even here the admiration by the critic is not so much for the ingenuity of applying musical technique to writing as for the gently satirical description of music itself. The creamy, dreamy tenderness of love music turns to the orgasm of "joygush" and "flood of warm jimjam lickitup secretness."[22] The high tenor note

[22] *Ibid.*, 270.

holds out until it soars higher and higher into the triteness of "the effulgence symbolistic," "the high vast irradiation," "the endless-nessnessness."[23] An air from *Martha* applies the inanity of opera language to a pun on Bloom's waiter: "Pat is a waiter who waits while you wait. Hee hee hee hee. He waits while you wait. Hee hee. A waiter is he. Hee hee hee hee. He waits while you wait. While you wait if you wait he will wait while you wait. Hee hee hee hee. Hoh. Wait while you wait."[24]

In creating the effect of music applied to words, Joyce plays many clever tricks. In addition to the variations in the main themes, he plays changes upon names themselves, for example Bloowho, Bloowhose, Bloohimwhom, Greaseabloom, wise Bloom. At one point love's old sweet song calls up a whole movement *andante con amore*, at another a penitential religious song leads to a sorrowful adagio, while the erotic mood is more like a scherzo. In the background the variations on bronze and gold set the mood as the barmaids react to the scene in front of them; for example, as a joke is told: "They threw young heads back, bronze gigglegold, to let freefly their laughter."[25] Along with the fugue and its variations, Joyce slips in other playful reminders of music, an amusing commentary on the resemblance between mathematics and music,[26] a bawdy explanation of "chamber music,"[27] and a burlesque of a vocal duet.[28] After the cleverness and occasional beauty of the development, Joyce ends the musical episode with a deliberate bit of cacophony that insults the reader's taste until he remembers that the ironic loneliness of Bloom's reading the Irish hero's last words as he relieves himself of diges-

[23] *Ibid.*, 271.
[24] *Ibid.*, 276.
[25] *Ibid.*, 256.
[26] *Ibid.*, 274.
[27] *Ibid.*, 278.
[28] *Ibid.*, 273.

tive gases combines with the bitter loneliness of the blind piano tuner and the futile gayety of the barmaids and singers to point up the unheroic search for happiness by modern man.

12. "The Cyclops." 5:00 P.M. Kiernan's saloon. This episode, like the preceding one, adds little to Bloom's story but contains some of Joyce's richest comic satire. Bloom goes to the saloon for an appointment with Martin Cunningham to confer about helping Paddy Dignam's widow, and while waiting gets into conversation with a rough bunch of half-drunk Irish patriots. Their boisterous nationalism becomes more noisy as Bloom becomes more tolerant in his attempt to present an unprejudiced point of view on various minor questions that come up. The ringleader is the unnamed "Citizen," whose gigantic bluster assails the modest Bloom even as the giant Cyclops, Polyphemus, in Homer's story attacks Ulysses. The Citizen's prejudices become anti-Semitic as Bloom abstains from drinking and hence from buying drinks for others. When Bloom leaves on an errand, the rumor goes around that he has gone secretly to collect his winnings from having bet on the dark horse in the Ascot Gold Cup. The prejudice is quickly fanned to unmeaning hatred, so that by the time Bloom returns to meet Cunningham he is attacked so violently that he barely escapes even with his friend's aid.

Meager as it is, the narrative content of this episode gives an excellent picture of the tolerant Bloom, who is nevertheless not afraid to answer the prejudiced arguments of the citizen. "I declare to my antimacassar," says the Narrator, "if you took up a straw from the bloody floor and if you said to Bloom: *Look at, Bloom. Do you see that straw? That's a straw.* Declare to my aunt he'd talk about it for an hour so he would and talk steady."[29]

[29] *Ibid.*, 311.

But the genius of Joyce is shown here most in the magnificent feast of parody and other kinds of comic satire. The technique is said to be "gigantism," which in this case means that the crude, earthy language of the Narrator is from time to time projected to tremendously inflated proportions like a movie seen from the front row. These lengthy parodies of every sort of jargon conceived by man may slow up the story, but at the same time they create an impression of satire that has hardly been equaled since Rabelais. In fact they remind one of Rabelais brought up to date, no longer poking fun at the pedantry and shallowness of medieval scholastic learning but at the shallowness and pedantry of the twentieth-century journalists, lawyers, scientific writers, society-page editors, sports writers, patriots, legislators, mystics, faith healers, and sentimental novelists. The windy gushiness of Ossian is not missed, and a brutal parody of the Apostles' Creed is thrown in for irreverent measure.

The style is that of Rabelais, or at least of the amazing translation of Rabelais by that seventeenth-century eccentric Scotsman, Sir Thomas Urquhart. Before one has read two pages, the grotesque profusion of synonyms and the fertile cataloguing of names and categories remind one forcibly of Gargantua, that progeny of Grangousier who believed in always doing things in a big way. Even to illustrate what I mean is impossible without taking parts of Gargantuan sentences that stretch away into paragraphs. For example, the mention of cattle recalls the fertility of the earth in bearing foodstuffs of all sorts, fishes, vegetables, fruits, and finally all kinds of edible animals: "and there is ever heard a trampling, cackling, roaring, lowing, bleating, bellowing, rumbling, grunting, champing, chewing, of sheep and pigs and heavyhooved kine from pasturelands of Lush and Rush and Carrick-mines," and so on.[30] The mention of heroes calls forth a list of nearly a page of Irishmen, which includes with the actual inhabitants such ringers as Franklin, Napoleon, Cleopatra, Thomas Cook and Son, William Tell, Buddha, Lady Godiva, and the Queen of Sheba.[31] In satirizing the ultrapatriotic Fenians, Joyce describes an animated altercation regarding whether the eighth or the ninth of March was the correct date of the birth of Ireland's patron saint. "In the course of the argument cannonballs, scimitars, boomerangs, blunderbusses, stinkpots, meatchoppers, umbrellas, catapults, knuckledusters, sandbags, lumps of pig iron were resorted to and blows were freely exchanged."[32] A detailed analysis of this episode follows in Chapter VI.

13. "Nausicaa." 8:00 P.M. Sandymount Beach. The first half of this episode alternates between the realistic account of trivial happenings and the sentimental story of Gerty MacDowell. Gerty and two other young girls have taken some children in their charge to the beach to play and to watch fireworks. Gerty's desires, depicted with all the sugary triteness of a sentimental novel, become centered on an older gentleman watching the girls; they reach a symbolic climax and merge with the erotic thoughts of Bloom (for it is he who is watching) as a skyrocket bursts high in the air. From this point the episode belongs to Bloom as he reviews nostalgically all the desires of love's old sweet song, oppressed by the weariness of advancing age, of early evening, and of the letdown that comes after the orgasm of passion. The episode is pathetic and tender, difficult to understand only when Bloom's regret

[30] *Ibid.*, 289.   [32] *Ibid.*, 302.
[31] *Ibid.*, 291.

for what he cannot recapture ties together all the themes that have been announced during the day.

14. "The Oxen of the Sun." 10:00 P.M. Maternity hospital in Holles Street. This episode, in which Bloom listens to the half-drunken talk of several rowdy young men, including Stephen, while he waits to hear about the delivery of Mrs. Purefoy, has been called an amazing tour de force. Its attempt to symbolize embryonic growth by a succession of parodies of the various stages of the English language and its literature is ingenious, it is true, but appalling. Its trickery is as satisfying to the literary as it is disturbing to a reader trying to follow the story of Bloom. It takes one on a bus ride through English literature much faster than does Mrs. Woolf's *Orlando*. Its erudition, especially in the evolutionary use of language, is at times annoying, yet its satire seldom fails to draw a laugh. It is an orgy of parody that at times approaches the grandeur of the original, as in the Swiftian tale of the papal bulls that grow fat upon Ireland, and at times flays the weakness of the original, as in the burlesque of sentimentality that suggests Dickens or the bombastic oratory that recalls Carlyle. It ends in a drunken burst of slang.

Although the style of this episode is ingeniously versatile, the narrative may be followed even when it is obscured by the archaisms intended to give the flavor of early English. The theme throughout is that of procreation and birth, a contrast with the thematic development of death in the "Hades" episode.[33] Bloom comes to Andrew Horne's maternity hospital in Holles Street to inquire about the expected delivery of Mrs. Purefoy. For a mo-

[33] A detailed analysis of this episode, showing how the development of language in England symbolizes embryonic growth, follows in Chapter VI.

ment he chats with a nurse about mutual acquaintances. A medical student, Dixon, whom he knew slightly, persuades him to join a group of carousing young men while he waits for news. Bloom cautiously takes a glass of ale but empties most of it in his neighbor's glass, so that he stays sober as the rest of the group gradually get more boisterous.

One by one the young men are introduced, as they talk about various problems tied in with birth, most frequently the bawdy aspects dealing with sexual relations. Besides Dixon there are his fellow-students Lynch and Madden, the jokester Lenehan already well known, the colorless Crotthers, the raucous Punch Costello, and the philosophical Stephen Dedalus. Bloom feels ill at ease with these drunken young men, but he stays on with them, partly out of weariness but mostly from loving solicitude for Stephen. When the group argue about whether a mother's life should be risked to save a child being born, Bloom's "wariness of mind" leads him to dissemble, "as his wont was," and he evades the question by a compromising answer. Bloom is reminded by the conversation of the death of his son when only eleven days old, and he looks upon Stephen with sadness because he had not "a son of such gentle courage" and because Stephen, whom he desires as a son, is wasting himself in riotous living.[34]

At this point Stephen fills all the cups around and proceeds in learned language to blaspheme the virgin birth and ridicule the vows of the Church. This leads to bawdy talk of wedding ceremonies, in the midst of which a thunderstorm breaks outside. Meanwhile, Buck Mulligan, who tortured Stephen early in the morning with his blunt taunts, arrives with Alec Bannon, whom

[34] *Ibid.*, 384.

he met on the way to the hospital. Mulligan is in a gay mood that makes him immediately a part of the hearty bawdiness. To prevent sterility and not to deprive females of their sexual rights, he offers himself as official "Fertilizer and Incubator." His hilarity and forthright masculinity contrast with Stephen's soft-spoken philosophizing. The conversation takes many turns, interspersed with Bloom's own meditations, until the successful delivery of Mrs. Purefoy is announced. The group breaks up as Stephen rushes out and Bloom follows, still wearing his black mourning clothes and trudging after Stephen.

15. "Circe." Midnight. In and near the brothel of Bella Cohen in the slum area of east Dublin. This episode is the high point of *Ulysses*. Longer by far than any of the other episodes (171 pages), it nevertheless moves very rapidly with the swift transformations one associates with dreams or with the movie theater. Indeed, its technique is much like that of a well-made modern movie, in which a minimum of talking is supplemented by good directing and skillful photography. The whole episode is written like a play with dialogue and stage directions, but the quick changes of scene, or rather of character within a scene, can only be reproduced in moving pictures.

The rapid transformations correspond only roughly to those brought about by Homer's enchantress Circe, who turns men into animals. These changes represent projected thoughts and Freudian desires which, under the stimulus of Stephen's liquor or of Bloom's excitement at going to the rescue of Stephen, tumble in rich profusion over one another. This long but exciting episode is an amazing medley of magic and fantasy that far outdoes the Walpurgis night scenes of Goethe's *Faust* with which it has been compared. It recapitulates, in terms of the events of the day, most of the conscious lives of Bloom and Stephen, and, more important still, it dramatizes with electric clearness their subconscious desires. "Circe" carries forward, of course, the main theme of *Ulysses*, the union of Bloom and Stephen, spiritual father and son. Incidentally, it contains the richest comic satire of a book that is full of Irish wit and comedy.

The episode is far too long and too complicated, in its rapidly shifting scenes, to be analyzed fully, and that is probably why critics have been inclined to dismiss it with relatively little comment. In Chapter Six, however, I have used a summary of Bloom's thoughts while talking to Zoe Higgins outside the brothel to illustrate the cinema technique of this episode. The first part transforms prosaic events of the day into fantastically colored projections of Bloom's innermost desires. The second part deals with the political rise and fall of Bloom the reformer, a masterpiece of satire on politicians and Irish blarney.

Meanwhile the narrative can be separated from the fantasy, though the story is here relatively unimportant. At first, Bloom has become separated from the drunken Stephen and his companion Lynch, but he follows them from a distance to Bella Cohen's brothel. Bloom talks to one of the whores, Zoe, and the dreams of his past bring about a bewildering series of transformations. He then enters the house to find Stephen playing the piano. The whoremistress Bella arrives, and under her masculine dominance Bloom becomes a cringing female; however, the spell is broken by the snapping of a back trousers' button. Stephen becomes too lavish with his money, and Bloom takes charge of it for him. Stephen, thinking about his mother, desperately smashes the chandelier and rushes from the house. Bella demands ten shillings for damages, but Bloom pays one shilling and follows Stephen. Outside Stephen gets into a brawl with two soldiers, and the police arrive, but Bloom with the help of a friend gets the police to make no report. The two are left alone on the street, and the amazing episode ends with Bloom standing beside the prostrate form of Stephen as the figure of the dead son Rudy appears in the guise of a fairy boy of eleven in an Eton suit.

The Homecoming.

16. "Eumaeus." 1:00 A.M. Cabman's shelter near Butt Bridge. With this episode the third and final section of *Ulysses* begins. This description of the walk from the brothel to Bloom's house is, intentionally, one of the worst written pieces of modern literature. In this episode practically every rule of English grammar is so deliberately broken that the instructor of Freshman composition longs to get out his red pencil for the first page or so and then gives up in despair, until at last, if he is so faithful, he revels in seeing how far Joyce can carry his howlers. Critics have made it clear that the loose style suggests the weariness of Stephen recovering from his drunk and from a knockout blow in a street brawl. Its very sprawling evokes in the reader an unclear mind, like a sort of hangover from the electric vividness of the preceding episode.

Even at the outset the sentences yawn and the phrases abound in clichés: "So far as he [Bloom] could see he [Stephen] was rather pale in the face so that it occurred to him as highly advisable to get a conveyance of some description which would answer in their then condition, both of them being e.d.ed, particularly Stephen, always assuming that there was such a thing to be found."[35]

A vague beginning and a weak ending are a suitable frame for a dangling participle and a mixed metaphor in this sentence: "This was a quandary but, bringing commonsense to bear on it, evidently there was nothing for it but put a good face on the matter and foot it which they accordingly did."[36] Circumlocution is abundant: "the recent visitation of Jupiter Pluvius," "the very palatable odour indeed of our daily bread, of all commodities of the public the primary and most indispensable,"[37] "bracing ozone," "the sights of the great metropolis, the spectacle of our modern Babylon,"[38] and numerous others.

Some of the sentences in this episode are so loosely constructed that they sprawl down half a page with all sorts of unrelated dependent clauses shooting off at odd angles. The best examples of these are too long to quote. Here is the beginning of one: "For instance, when the evicted tenants' question, then at its first inception, bulked largely in people's minds though, it goes without saying, not contributing a copper or pinning his faith absolutely to its dictums, some of which wouldn't exactly hold water, he at the outset in principle, at all events, was in thorough sympathy with peasant possession, as voicing the trend of modern opinion, a partiality, however, which, realizing his mistake, he was subsequently partially cured of, and even was twitted with going a step further than Michael Davitt in the striking views he at one time inculcated as a backtothelander, which was one reason he

[35] *Ibid.*, 597. [37] *Ibid.*, 598.
[36] *Ibid.* [38] *Ibid.*, 611.

strongly resented the innuendo put upon him in so barefaced a fashion . . ." and so on through three more dependent clauses and several digressive phrases to a beautifully climactic phrase, "in a word."[39] As a contribution to the comic satire of *Ulysses*, the best part of this episode is the array of trite phrases and proverbial sayings that produce mixed metaphors, as in "his erstwhile staunch adherents and his beloved evicted tenants for whom he had done yeoman service in the rural parts of the country by taking up the cudgels on their behalf in a way that exceeded their most sanguine expectations, very effectually cooked his matrimonial goose, thereby heaping coals of fire on his head, much in the same way as the fabled ass's kick."[40] Surely it takes a master of English to butcher his native language with such deliberate effectiveness.

In spite of the loose construction of sentences, episode sixteen is not hard to read, partly because the narrative runs on in the incoherent manner of a person who starts talking about one subject and is suddenly reminded of something else. Furthermore, the first part describes very realistically the conversation of several low-life characters in the shelter. Indeed, some of the scenes are unforgettable, like that of sailor Murphy wrinkling his hairy skin to make the tattooed figure change while the cabmen crowd round to admire. And when Murphy illustrates one of his stories of prowess with a fierce-looking knife, the reader feels as ready as Bloom to do as little as possible to arouse his anger.

In the latter part of the episode, however, even while the style becomes more sprawling, we see the pathetic attempts of

[39] *Ibid.*, 641.
[40] *Ibid.*, 635.

Bloom to interest Stephen as he gradually comes out of his intoxicated state. Bloom hovers over the young man, brings him coffee and food, shows him pictures of his wife Molly, and suggests all sorts of ways of making money, including singing duets on the concert stage with Molly, but Stephen appears indifferent, even when he goes with Bloom out into the streets and listens to warnings against Mulligan. For example, when Bloom suggests that a walk in the night air would do them good and nimbly skips around on the right, passing his left arm in Stephen's right, and leading him on, the young man is almost hostile from the feeling of the differences between them in age, race, and manner of thinking: " 'Yes,' Stephen said uncertainly, because he thought he felt a strange kind of flesh of a different man approach him, sinewless and wobbly and all that."[41]

17. "Ithaca." 2:00 A.M. Bloom's kitchen. Even as Ulysses in the old story comes home to the island of Ithaca to meet his son Telemachus, so Bloom takes Stephen home with him late at night and makes a cup of cocoa for him while they talk things over and plan for the future. The episode is in the form of an elaborate catechism that seems, at first, even more stupid than the "Eumaeus" episode. The history in it is given with precise and pedantic exactness; the philosophy is often obscured unnecessarily; and the science, which is here very prominent, is accompanied by mathematical formulae and technical words. But if the reader feels inclined to skip this section because of its scientific manner, let him beware. For in this catechism Joyce has summarized his story and thrown in a picture of the complexity of modern life for good measure.

[41] *Ibid.*, 644.

In the first place this episode contains the climax of the story itself, Bloom's adoption of Stephen and his decision to assert his rights with the erring Molly. Behind the catechism the narrative appears plainly enough: Bloom climbs the areaway railing and enters by the back door because he has left his key; he lets Stephen in by the hallway; the two talk together about many things; Bloom returns Stephen's money and makes plans for him to give Italian lessons to Molly and to receive voice lessons from her; Stephen finally takes his leave after declining the offer to stay all night; and Bloom undresses and goes to bed in an agitated state of mind, boldly waking Molly and talking to her of the day's events, especially of Stephen.

But the events are trivial compared with the variety and the mass of the information provided. Here are the clues to Bloom's past life and present desires, the very fiber of his character. The differences between Stephen's intellectual (artistic) nature and Bloom's practical (scientific) nature are explored beyond the obvious unlikenesses of name, age, race, and creed; and the similarities of reluctance to shed human blood and of the "firm full masculine feminine passive active hand" are implied in different ways. Underneath all the prosaic catechism appears Bloom's nobler side in his desire to "amend many social conditions, the product of inequality and avarice and international animosity."[42]

But there is more in this episode than the answer of Everyman Bloom, who has traveled far in his mind's eye and now comes to rest beside the warm body of Molly. Out of all these dry answers comes the answer, if any, to the eternal riddle of our complex modern life, the compromise between restlessness and inertia, be-

[42] *Ibid.*, 681.

tween idealism and the practicable, between the desire for luxury and the necessity of poverty, between promiscuous lasciviousness and love of family life, between the complications of modern life brought about by science and the vast stretching universe revealed by science. And incidentally there are poetic moments, such as the scientific hymn to water[43] and the twin prose poems of the telescopic and the microscopic universes.[44]

18. "Penelope." 2:45 A.M. Bloom's bedroom. Joyce turns in this final episode to the resolving of his theme, returning all thought to the earth whence it came, allowing Molly Bloom, who is the very essence of earthy fertility, to have the last say in unpunctuated reverie that easily merges into dreams or dreamless sleep. Molly's thoughts, while they flow on without pause except for seven unnecessary breaks, do not require any punctuation; their everyday homeliness, mixed with occasional frank obscenity, makes them perhaps the most easily understood of all Joyce's writings. For the episode is disarmingly simple, or as Joyce wrote to his friend Budgen, "sane full amoral."

Of course Molly does not know that Leopold has put down the suitors by his very equanimity in reflecting that each suitor, including the most recent Boylan, imagined himself "to be first, last, only and alone, whereas he is neither first nor last nor only nor alone in a series originating in and repeated to infinity."[45] She is at first bewildered by Leopold's assertion of his rights, symbolized in his usual compromising manner by an unusual kiss and by a request for his breakfast in bed the next morning. Unable to sleep, she thinks of a thousand everyday things—the vexation be-

[43] *Ibid.*, 655.   [45] *Ibid.*, 716.
[44] *Ibid.*, 683.

cause her daughter Milly is so much like her, domestic details of servants and cooking and the gynecologist with his highbrow medical terms. Of course, sexual thoughts intrude from time to time—as they must because of her latest affair that very afternoon, because she is physically upset by woman's period coming on, and because she is the full-bodied female that she is. These are the salacious details the reader remembers but they typify what is relatively only one of many important parts of her life. Even the memories of former lovers assume the significance they deserve: the only one fully described is the puppy love with Mulvey that was never consummated, and the stallion-like Boylan is already replaced in her desires by the prospect of taking on the youthful and unsuspecting Stephen Dedalus.

The whole episode begins and ends with the word *yes*, and the idea beats out a steady refrain throughout all her thoughts. No wonder Joyce describes Molly, in his letter to Budgen, as the symbol of affirmation by paraphrasing Goethe's line, in which Mephistopheles tells Faust he is the spirit that continually denies (*"Ich bin der Geist der stets verneint"*). Molly is, on the contrary, the flesh that always affirms by saying yes (*"Ich bin der Fleisch der stets bejaht"*).

It is significant, however, that Bloom is the last one in her thoughts. The planned seduction of Stephen merges into a rosy reverie of youthful love scenes that ends with the enthusiastic affirmation of Bloom's proposal to her on Howth hill, the idyllic scene from love's old sweet song that Bloom has tried during the day to recapture: "and I thought well as well him as another and then I asked him with my eyes to ask again yes and then he asked me would I yes to say yes my mountain flower and first I put my arms around him yes and drew him down to me so he could feel my breasts all perfume yes and his heart was going like mad and yes I said yes I will Yes."[46]

[46] *Ibid.*, 768.

CHAPTER SIX

SPECIAL TECHNIQUES IN ULYSSES

Many readers have found *Ulysses* good fun, always exciting to the imagination, and at times even moving. They may have marked some parts of it for more careful study. They need not feel that further study means going immediately to the symbolism, the Homeric parallels, and those other paraphernalia of organs, arts, and colors that are so dear to the Joyce cult. If they want guideposts to such esoteric knowledge, they can find them in many books, especially in the writings of Stuart Gilbert and Frank Budgen, both of whom talked and corresponded with Joyce. But there is still much to be learned and enjoyed in *Ulysses* without becoming burdened with symbolism. It is in this further enjoyment of the work that I should like to help the curious reader.

There are two qualities in *Ulysses* that have excited me to the point of sending me back to read it time after time. The first of these—and the one that appeals to any linguist—is Joyce's mastery of words. The second is his mastery of comic effect, ranging from the good-humored laughter that belongs to the vaudeville stage through the parody of literary styles to the powerful punches of devastating satire. These two qualities are exciting because Joyce himself found them exciting. He sometimes pushed them so far in his excitement that he almost lost sight of his main theme. In other words, Joyce occasionally got so interested in the special technique he used for every episode in *Ulysses* that the result no longer resembles fiction. When this happens, the special technique needs special explanation. Let me illustrate what I mean.

There are episodes in *Ulysses* where technique appears to swallow story and characters alike, as in those at the library and at the maternity hospital. There are still other episodes where technique momentarily obscures the main theme but finally recovers it and gives it an emphasis that would otherwise have been lost, as in the "Aeolus," "Nausicaa," and "Sirens" episodes. Most interesting of all, however, are those episodes where technique and matter are inextricably bound together, where the special technique employed has the air of novelty that soon gives way to directness and the power to develop character and theme.

Such happy combinations of technique and story are tributes to Joyce's perfect artistry, even though some of them may seem dull on first sight. For example, in the "Eumaeus" episode, the mood to be suggested is the dullness of weary minds in a cabmen's shelter late at night. Again, in the "Ithaca" episode, the story gives way to intricate weaving of themes that must not be missed and so are rehearsed like a catechism by the two chief characters in Bloom's kitchen. On the other hand, when the happy combination appears in those parts of the book where the story calls for vigor and vividness, the episodes are the high points of *Ulysses*. Powerful expressions of the artist's creative skill, they are still so packed with meaning and expressed in so new a medium that they need more than the casual explanation I have given in the general analysis of the preceding chapter.

Two examples, included here, of this kind of episode in *Ulysses* are the "Cyclops" and "Circe" episodes, brilliant chapters that deserve special study. To them I have added "The Oxen of the Sun," the episode in which bawdy young men talk about gestation at the maternity hospital, partly because it appeals to my background in linguistics and partly because I think critics have been too harsh in calling it an artificial tour de force. I should like to add others, but there is a limit to what the common reader will bear, and besides I have given at least clues to them in Chapter Five.

"The Cyclops" *(episode 12)*

Joyce says that he is using in this episode the technique of "gigantism" to suggest the ancient giant Polyphemus, the one-eyed Cyclops who harassed and almost killed Ulysses. In my brief analysis of this episode in Chapter Five I have shown how this gigantism produces a style that closely resembles that of Rabelais with its gargantuan piling up of synonyms and its lusty search for the strange but vivid word to fit the situation.

Another resemblance of Joyce to Rabelais, that will appear in the detailed analysis below, is in the powerful use of sidesplitting comedy for purposes of satire. Like Rabelais, Joyce lashes at the futility and decadence of his age. Where Rabelais laughed away the empty remains of medieval scholasticism, Joyce holds up to ridicule the complex riddle of modern life. Like Rabelais, Joyce uses comedy for serious purposes, to let the air out of the inflated jargon and pretentiousness, to expose the barren wastes of man's desires, and to make men laugh at their own follies.

The technique of gigantism, as I have suggested, is to inflate simple ideas and statements from the conversation in Kiernan's saloon until they become like great, colored toy balloons ready to be punctured. In my analysis of the episode, space is saved by using a modified tabular form: (1) page references to identify each passage; (2) summary of the simple narrative statement or event; and (3) summary of the inflated form, with examples to illustrate comic methods.

287–88.   The report of a conversation involving the attempt of a Jewish merchant to collect three shillings a week for payment of goods furnished becomes inflated to a wordy contract in legal jargon, typified by the conclusion: "as this day hereby agreed between the said vendor, his heirs, successors, trustees and assigns of the one part and the said purchaser, his heirs, successors, trustees and assigns of the other part."

288–90.   The attempt of an Irishman to forestall his legitimate debt to Moses Herzog becomes inflated to two pages of exalted description of Irish provision merchants done in the wordy and sentimental manner of Ossian, accentuated by the piling up of synonyms or lists of names in the style of Rabelais. Nine kinds of fish sport in the murmuring waters of Inisfail the fair, besides "the mixed coarse fish generally and other denizens of the aqueous kingdom too numerous to be enumerated." Among other things, a produce market is described as a shining palace with a "crystal glittering roof," to which "the extremely large wains bring foison of the fields, flaskets of cauliflowers, floats of spinach, . . . spherical potatoes and tallies of irridescent kale, York and Savoy," and so on through the mellifluous triteness of other vegetables and fruits. Nineteen kinds of animals come to market "from pasturelands of

Lush and Rush and Carrickmines" and other epic-sounding parts of Ireland.

291–92.   The anonymous Narrator of the episode turns into Barney Kiernan's saloon to discover the anonymous Citizen, "waiting for what the sky would drop in the way of drink." The terse remarks of the Citizen show him to be an ultrapatriotic Fenian, a suitable medium for Joyce's satire of Irish nationalism as well as a goad for the tolerant Bloom who enters later. The Citizen is accompanied by "a savage animal of the canine tribe," suitably named Garryowen. The description of the Citizen becomes inflated to grandiose proportions suited to the hero of Irish epics, though in specific details he is more like the giants and ogres found in some of the medieval romances derived from Irish epics: "The widewinged nostrils, from which bristles of the same tawny hue projected, were of such capaciousness that within their cavernous obscurity the fieldlark might easily have lodged her nest." Sixteen compounded epithets describe his general appearance, and from his girdle hang eighty-seven tribal images of Irish heroes and heroines of antiquity. This magnificent list is headed by Cuchulin and a few other genuine figures, but continues in burlesque manner with Napoleon, Lady Godiva, Buddha, Patrick W. Shakespeare, the Man that Broke the Bank at Monte Carlo, and Jack the Giant Killer. Rabelais himself would have been proud of this mixture of Ossianic cloudiness, Gargantuan catalogues, and sharp satire on ancient sentiment and modern Fenianism.

292–95.   This passage contains several parallels to Homeric epic, particularly to Homer as he was known in the Victorian translations that were popular when Joyce was writing *Ulysses*.

The first is a reference to Bloom, still outside: "Who comes through Michan's land, bedight in sable armor? O'Bloom, the son of Rory: it is he. Impervious to fear is Rory's son: he of the prudent soul." The ridiculous figure of Dennis Breen, with lawbooks under his arm, followed by his wife, is described in the style of Homeric epic: "an elder of noble gait and countenance, bearing the sacred scrolls of law and with him his lady wife, a dame of peerless lineage, fairest of her race." The Homeric parody is continued in the brewing of ale, "the foaming ebon ale which the noble twin brothers Bungiveagh and Bungardilaun brew ever in their divine alevats, cunning as the sons of deathless Leda"; in the odd use of the second person found in Homer's *Odyssey* (in the passages dealing with swineherd Eumaeus): "Then did you, chivalrous Terence, hand forth, as to the manner born, that nectareous beverage"; and in the description of Queen Victoria on a bronze coin similar to the detailed pictures found on Achilles' shield in Homer's *Iliad*.

296.   Alf Bergan's mention of having just seen Paddy Dignam, not knowing he had been buried that morning, is inflated to a very comical picture of Dignam's spirit sending a message to his son about mending a pair of old shoes. The passage satirizes spiritualism, astrology, and the mystical cult of Hindu philosophy then fashionable in Dublin. A good example is Paddy's answer to the question whether life after death resembles life in this world: "he stated that he had heard from more favoured beings now in the spirit that their abodes were equipped with every modern comfort such as talafana, alavatar, hatakalda, wataklasat."

297.   The mourning for Dignam satirizes Irish sentiment in words that might have come right from the poems of Ossian

as they appeared in the so-called translations of the eighteenth-century James Macpherson: "He is gone from mortal haunts: O'Dignam, sun of our morning. Fleet was his foot on the bracken: Patrick of the beamy brow. Wail, Banba, with your wind: and wail, O ocean, with your whirlwind."

298–300. Bloom enters just in time to hear a letter from a hangman crudely describing his professional skill. Bloom is offered a drink but declines, accepting a cigar instead. The Narrator comments here and several times later on Bloom's prudence in not wishing to take sides. The parallel of cautious Bloom to Homer's crafty Odysseus and the symbol of the cigar as the burning stick with which Odysseus blinds the one-eyed giant Cyclops have been frequently noted. The profession of the hangman, master barber, is inflated to a short passage in bogus epic style about "the vengeful knights of the razor." Talk of the hanging leads to an explanation, in exaggerated scientific jargon, of why the penis of a hanged man becomes erect.

300–305. Further talk of hanging leads to that of Irish patriots who have been executed for the cause, whereupon the Citizen launches into a patriotic spiel, and Bloom, cautious, tries to take a compromising middle stand. The Citizen glares at Bloom and proposes a toast to the memory of the dead and to *Sinn Fein*. Bloom tries to explain his point, but the patriotic tidal wave overwhelms him. The Citizen's toast to the friends we love who are by our side is inflated to five pages of patriotic gush in trite journalistic jargon, culminating in a saccharine account of the touching farewell scene between a young patriot about to be executed and his love. The delegation of friends of the Emerald Isle, who witness the execution, consists of representatives of various nationalities whose names sound as if they were from a Gilbert and Sullivan opera or the latest vaudeville; the list ends with the German, *Kriegfried Ueberallgemein*, whose learned title is one word two lines long. The delegates fight over whether the eighth or ninth of March was the correct date of the birth of Ireland's patron saint. The execution does not take place, but the preparations are described, first with a mixture of foreign languages reminiscent of Rabelais' Panurge, then with the realism of horror fiction, then with the extravagant sentimentality of a love story, and finally with the smooth clichés of a society editor, whereupon even the stern provostmarshal, brushing away a furtive tear with his mailed gauntlet, was heard to say, "God blimey if she aint a clinker, that there bleeding tart."

306–307. The story of the Citizen talking to his dog in Irish is inflated to a satire on literary criticism, in which is extolled the cultural accomplishment of this remarkable dog reciting Irish verse. The platitudes of criticism are there: "A *striking* resemblance (the italics are ours) to the ranns of ancient Celtic bards"; "delightful lovesongs," "satirical effusions," "topical allusions," and "the metrical system of the canine original, which recalls the intricate alliterative and isosyllabic rules of the Welsh englyn."

308. Bob Doran's drunken sympathy for Mrs. Dignam is inflated to profuse jargon burlesquing false sentiment.

310. The news that Nannetti is to ask a question in the English Parliament about forbidding Irish games in the park is inflated to satire on legislative jargon in the style that might be used by the official journal of the House of Commons.

311–12. Discussion of the revival of ancient Gaelic sports is inflated to a verbose account of a meeting that ends with the singing of an Irish song. The meeting is described in clichés, such as "the venerable president of this noble order," "superlative form," and "stentorian notes." The clergy, the press, the bar, and other learned professions are in the audience. Twenty-four members of the clergy are listed by name and abbreviation of their order or degree (many of the abbreviations are unusual for the clergy), but all others are lumped in one brief statement: "The laity included P. Fay, T. Quirke, etc., etc."

313. Alf Bergan's concise slang account of a boxing match is inflated to a magnificent burlesque of a newspaper sports story.

314. Mention of Molly Bloom leads to a short description of her as if she were a heroine out of Ossian, beginning "Pride of Calpe's rocky mount, the ravenhaired daughter of Tweedy."

317. A case of law in which a Jew failed to get judgment against an Irish swindler is inflated to a pompous account of a jury trial in Biblical style mixed with legal jargon. The jury is described as "the high sinhedrim of the twelve tribes of Iar," that is, of Patrick, Hugh, Owen, Conn, Oscar, Fergus, Finn, Dermot, Cormac, Kevin, Caolte, and Ossian.

319–20. The entrance of Nolan and Lenehan leads to drunken abuse of the English for their treatment of the Irish. Two passages are inflated to read like old epics, one where "O'Nolan, clad in shining armor" describes a meeting on the revival of the ancient Irish language, the other a curse on the English: "uttering his tribal slogan *Lamh Dearg Abu*, he drank to the undoing of his foes." This is followed by an oratorical outburst by the Citizen on the departed glory of Ireland, brought low by the foe of mankind, "the yellowjohns of Anglia."

321–22. The Citizen's impassioned plea to save Ireland's

trees from devastation is inflated to a lengthy and very amusing account of the wedding of Miss Fir Conifer of Pine Valley, written as an extravagant parody of the jargon used by newspaper society editors. Allusions to forestry are woven into the description, including a list of twenty-nine names based on trees.

323. A conversation on the brutal methods of the British Navy is summed up in a parody of the Apostles' Creed.

326. Bloom has been laughed at for talking about the injustice that arises from national hatred. The overzealous Irish nationalism is inflated to a sentimental description of the glories of Ireland's past. A list of thirty-three famous places of Ireland includes Guinness's brewery, a workhouse, a jail, a bog, a warehouse, the three birthplaces of the first Duke of Wellington, St. Patrick's Purgatory, and Fingal's Cave: "all these moving scenes are still there for us today rendered more beautiful still by the waters of sorrow which have passed over them and by the rich incrustations of time."

328. Talk of English religious hypocrisy is inflated into a news story in pompous journalese describing a Zulu chief being presented to the leading cotton magnate of Manchester.

330. The arrival of Martin Cunningham at the saloon is described in a parody of early modern English as if it were a scene from Thomas Malory's *Morte d'Arthur*. Numerous archaic words give a humorous flavor, for example, *rustic hostelry, palfrey, varlet, saucy knave, sirrah, lackaday, larder, cry mercy, trencherman, collops of venison, flagon of old Rhenish.*

332–34. The intolerance of the Irishmen in the saloon, shown in their unreasoning hatred of the Jew because they misunderstand Bloom's reason for leaving the tavern, is covered up by a reference to patriotic religion. St. Patrick is invoked to return and rid Ireland of this new contamination. Cunningham's attempt to curb violence by saying, "God bless all here is my prayer," is inflated to the description of a gigantic religious procession that is almost unbelievable: crucifer; seven categories of helpers; five kinds of dignitaries with monks and friars named and described; "all saints and martyrs, virgins and confessors," eighty by name; and 11,000 virgins. The names of the saints are mostly Irish or those best known in Ireland, but they also include "S. Anonymous and S. Eponymous and S. Synonymous," as well as "Brother Aloysius Pacificus and Brother Louis Bellicosus." The "blessed symbols of the efficacies" woven into the robes of these saints number thirty-seven, including babes in a bathtub, buckshot, boxes of vaseline, watertight boats, eyes on a dish, and unicorns. The saints perform miracles as they march to Kiernan's saloon to bless it, and the ceremonies are described in a profuse parody of theological jargon. This passage is perhaps nearest the spirit and style of Rabelais of any in *Ulysses*.

335. Bloom returns and goes off again with Cunningham, followed by the drunken curses of the intolerant Citizen. The departure of the horse-drawn vehicle is described in poetic language like a parody of Shakespeare's description of Cleopatra's barge in *Antony and Cleopatra*.

336–37. The departure of Bloom is described in platitudes reminiscent of a sentimental novel and a small-town newspaper: "Amid cheers that rent the welkin, . . . the mastodonic pleasure-ship slowly moved away saluted by a final floral tribute from the representatives of the fair sex."

337–38. The noise and confusion as the drunken Citizen,

in a rage at Bloom, throws a biscuit tin at him is inflated to a parody of scientific writing: "From the reports of eyewitnesses it transpires that the seismic waves were accompanied by a violent atmospheric perturbation of cyclonic character."

339. The realism of the final escape of Bloom from the Fenian Cyclops is inflated to the apocalypse of Bloom ascending to heaven like Elijah, told like an Old Testament story.

George Meredith's statement that the essence of the comic spirit is incongruity has seldom been better illustrated than in these final scenes of the "Cyclops" episode. The meek little man, the very spirit of tolerance and willingness to compromise in order to keep peace, has turned when crowded too far and has openly confronted his persecutors. The ridiculous picture of the Citizen's futile rage and the little weak man become a sort of new Messiah is comic indeed, and yet it is a fitting conclusion for a chapter in which Joyce has satirized intolerance and prejudice and jingoism in general, and Irish nationalism and anti-Semitic feeling in particular. Joyce's favorite satirical method of burlesque and parody also holds up to ridicule all sorts of jargon, wordiness, triteness, and inflated style. The playful style has become more evident as the serious theme develops.

"The Oxen of the Sun" (episode 14)

This episode is an amazing example of linguistic virtuosity, in which Joyce deliberately symbolizes embryonic development by a rapid succession of passages that suggest the development of language in England. The changing style does not obscure the action which centers around the drunken conversation of several young bachelors who sit and joke about the sexual urge and its consequences, their unproductiveness contrasting with the fertility of mothers giving birth to children nearby. Indeed, the very language used is often what a group of intellectuals in their cups might use, paraphrasing the tags of older authors as they pop up in the memory.

Joyce explained what he was trying to do in a letter to Frank Budgen from Trieste, March 2, 1920, written while he was working on this episode.[1] In this letter he says he was using the technique of "a nine-parted episode without divisions introduced by a Sallustian-Tacitean prelude." He mentions the names of some English authors whose style he was parodying to represent the progress of language, virtually the same names that appear in the analyses of Stuart Gilbert and Frank Budgen, except for the nineteenth-century authors who appear simply as "Landor-Pater-Newman." "This progression" continues Joyce, "is also linked back at each part subtly with some foregoing episode of the day and besides this, with the natural stages of development of the embryo, and the periods of formal evolution in general."

Joyce had not finished writing the episode at the time of the letter, but in general the finished work resembles his plan: he was always linking later episodes with earlier ones, and the symbolism

[1] The letter, now in the Slocum collection at Yale University, was quoted by A. M. Klein in his meticulous study of the "Oxen of the Sun" in *Here and Now: a Canadian Quartely of Literature and Art*, Vol. I (1929), 28–48. My analysis was made before I saw Mr. Klein's overmeticulous commentary on the parallel with embryonic development and periods of evolution. Since it is the purpose of my book to rescue the reader of *Ulysses* from such elaborate exegesis, I have not altered my simple critical analysis of the episode.

of embryonic development is quite clear, though the parallel with periods of evolution is only vaguely suggested. In my opinion, the technique he uses is that of linguistic development and my analysis attempts to show clearly the stages, six periods that linguists might recognize after the "prelude." My fifth, sixth, and seventh stages could easily be divided to make the nine parts that Joyce suggests, if one wished to follow the original plan literally.

In short, Joyce has combined, in the maternity hospital episode, the realistic chatter of young intellectuals with the symbolism of embryo and evolution depicted by the development of language. The occasional resemblance to well-known English authors is inevitable because these writers themselves typify a phase of the development of language, but it seems clear to me that he was grouping authors to represent changing styles rather than parodying individuals. Too much emphasis has been put on this episode as a series of parodies of English authors. Joyce never wasted an opportunity to ridicule jargon and bogus sentiment, it is true, but here, as in the "Cyclops" episode, the literary satire is merely a part of a larger purpose. My analysis, from a linguistic point of view, of the various stages by which Joyce depicts the evolution of language in England, will show what I mean.

The first stage in the development of language belongs to the primitive state of mankind symbolized by magic and revealed by folklore survivals. This is revealed in three brief incantations, each repeated the magical three times, the first in mixed Latin and Gaelic, the second in words from early English, the third in plain shouts of joy that might be modern slang.

The second stage (377–78) is the chaotic jumble of words with no punctuation and with the barest of syntax or orderly thought, what Joyce calls "a Sallustian-Tacitean prelude (the un-fertilized ovum)." Out of this welter of phrases, ideas swim to the surface from time to time, and indeed if we read the first para-graph aloud we can see that the word order is that of the classical Latin used in Roman Britain. For example, if we omit certain modifying phrases, we can read the first six lines of the paragraph as a fairly lucid statement: "Universally that person's acumen is esteemed very little perceptive . . . who is ignorant of that which the most . . . erudite and . . . deserving of veneration constantly maintain." Word order that seems barbarous in English would be common in classical Latin, for example, "the most in doctrine erudite" or "that in them high mind's ornament." The next two paragraphs gradually introduce punctuation and more normal word order, but the vocabulary is still dominantly Latin in origin.

Then comes the third stage (378–79), the Old English pe-riod, at first with a mixture of native words and Latinized diction, then with the dominant Anglo-Saxon vocabulary and rhythm. The first phase is announced by two lines of alliterative poetry that have the same two beats to the half-line that are found in *Beowulf*. Then the Anglo-Saxon flavor gives way to Latin for a few lines, until the full force of native words is resumed with de-liberate use of archaic diction and frequent alliteration. Obsolete words are revived: *thole* (suffer), *twey* (two), *eft* (again), *swire* (neck), *levin* (lightning), *rood* (cross), *rathe* (soon), and *wot-ting* (knowing). Expressions typical only of Anglo-Saxon gram-mar or style are invented: *there* (for where), *so* (for as), *bed-thanes* (for nurses), *ywimpled* (old form for past participle), *on got* (for perceived, from the past tense of A. S. *ongietan*) and *infare* (for enter). Numerous archaic words are brought in for flavor because they were common in early English: *teeming, want, bairns, hale, quoth, welkin, wreaker, loth, stow, ere, doffed,* and *swart.*

The fourth stage (379–84) represents the transition from Middle English to Early Modern English, roughly the fourteenth and fifteenth centuries. In these pages there are definite allusions to certain writings of the period, to the morality plays ("Everyman look to that last end that is thy death"), to the romances in Malory ("Childe Leopold" and "the learning knight yclept Dixon"), to the fabulous travels of Mandeville (table, knives, glass, and a dish of sardines described as if they were magical), to the early theological controversies (if one of the two must die, should it be mother or child?), and finally to the simple language of early translations of the Bible that culminated in the King James version (Leopold's sorrow for the loss of his son and his yearning to adopt Stephen).

Again Joyce in these passages is more concerned with giving the flavor of pre-Shakespearean English than in parodying Malory or any other author. Some of the more obvious archaisms come naturally from Malory, for his *Morte d'Arthur* is about the only work of the fifteenth century still known to modern readers. As in the early period, however, the flavor comes from archaic words, at first mainly native words but increasingly weighted by the introduction of Latin and French words: *grameful, algate, withsay, wanhope, wend, mickle, of his avis, trow, wight, natheless, emprise, meseems, quaff, orgulous, aver, eftsoons, maugre, jocund, deliverly* (agilely). Again, too, Joyce deliberately digs out obsolete words and phrases to emphasize the early stage in the development of the English language: *unneth* (difficult), *was died, was come,*

three year agone come childermass, never was none so hard, couth
(known), *sithen* (since), *by cause* (because), *was smitten* (incorrect analogy with *was died*), *did do make* (caused to be made),
otherwhither, ne (nor), *halp* (helped), *nist not* (knew not, with
double negative), *our alther* (of us all), *hight, clepen* (call, name),
ruth red him (pity encouraged him), *aresouns* (reasons), *an* (if),
and or I err (unless I err).

The fifth stage (384–91) represents the Early Modern English of the sixteenth and seventeenth centuries. Again there are reminiscences of the simple but dignified style of the King James Bible, of the more grandiose and somewhat Latinized style of Sir Thomas Browne or John Milton, and of the realistic style of Elizabethan tales and comedies. There is an allusion to Beaumont and Fletcher's *Maid's Tragedy*, followed by a bawdy pun in the Elizabethan manner. There are also at least two conscious parodies. The first, ironically, describes the wanton lasciviousness of the young men in the allegory and simple language of Bunyan's *Pilgrim's Progress:* "Yes, Pious had told him of that land and Chaste had pointed him to the way but the reason was that in the way he fell in with a certain whore of an eyepleasing exterior whose name, she said, is Bird-in-the-Hand." The second parody reflects the earthy realism, packed meaning, and fast action of Samuel Pepys's famous diary, as it retells the events of the day that has just passed, for example: "Leopold Bloom there for a languor he had but was now better, he having dreamed tonight a strange fancy of his dame Mrs. Moll with red slippers on in a pair of Turkey trunks."

Except for the two parodies, the rest of this section is a mélange of Elizabethan style, a mixture of puns and great poetry, of slang and noble English and Latin phrases and aureate ink-horn terms, of versatile swearing and exalted worship. The nobility of the prose of Sir Thomas Browne may be seen in these words, even when the borrowings from Blake and Yeats are recognized: "Time's ruins build eternity's mansions. What means this? Desire's wind blasts the thorntree but after it becomes from a bramble bush to be a rose upon the rood of time." Any number of low-life characters in Elizabethan comedy might have said, "Thou chuff, thou puny, thou got in the peasestraw, thou losel, thou chitterling, thou spawn of a rebel, thou dyke dropt, thou abortion thou." The despair of the Psalmist is reflected in these poetic phrases: "And thou hast left me alone for ever in the dark ways of my bitterness: and with a kiss of ashes hast thou kissed my mouth." Yet the same Elizabethan era could proliferate such bookish abominations as these: "That same multiplicit concordance which leads forth growth from birth accomplishing by a retrogressive metamorphosis that minishing and ablation towards the final."

All this mixture of heaven and earth is part of the vigorous and youthful spirit of the Elizabethans, that strange striving which Joyce is trying to present in terms of an era rather than of individual writers. It is difficult in any other way to find a common denominator for Spenser, Shakespeare, Marlowe, Jonson, Donne, Browne, Burton, and dozens of other writers just as varied. Joyce tries instead to capture the spirit of the age, and he does it more successfully than with the earlier stages of the language, because he is now in familiar territory.

The sixth stage (391–405) represents Modern English of the classical eighteenth century, tapering off at the end into the extravagances of the romantic era. The great prose of the early eighteenth century has in it a combination of realistic narrative, concise diction, and well-chosen vocabulary that does not lend itself to ridicule. Instead of parody Joyce has here imitated the original style with the result that he has achieved somewhat the same effect as Defoe and Swift. The conversation of Stephen and his companions about cows being killed because of disease has the flavor of Defoe's journalistic pen, but the ensuing story of Stephen about the papal bulls of farmer Nicholas and the chicanery of the lord Harry in Ireland is so well told in Jonathan Swift's manner that it might be an episode in A *Tale of a Tub*.

Inspired by Stephen's brilliance, Buck Mulligan proposes to aid the human race by becoming "Fertiliser and Incubator" for all unattached females. The easy narrative and the lewd comments inspired by this proposal are much in the manner of Steele and Addison, but when the Scottish student brings out a locket from his bosom and gushes with a sort of leering lasciviousness we can imagine we are reading from Sterne's *Sentimental Journey*. The general hilarity that follows is a mixture of realistic, bawdy talk and high-flown sentiment, a contrast not too different from that found frequently in the eighteenth-century novels of Henry Fielding and Samuel Richardson.

As the action progresses, this mixture is further supplemented with the dignified classical diction, the sonorous periods, and the Latin phrases reminiscent of Samuel Johnson and Edmund Burke, used by Joyce to express the more serious rejoinders of Leopold Bloom as he tries to refute the bawdy young men. In passages like these it is futile to try to recognize individual authors, for the whole mixture of realism and sentiment and seriousness are found side-by-side in many writers of the latter part of the eighteenth century. It is equally futile to recognize individuals in the hodgepodge of legal and scientific jargon used to comment on the announced birth of a son to Mrs. Purefoy, for the passage is an imitation of many popular books that reflect the growing interest in scientific discoveries. The transition to the nineteenth century comes in this scene and in the horror scene based on "Malachias' Tale," where all the fantastic trappings and trickery of the Gothic novel are paraded in one short paragraph: the secret panel beside the chimney, the poison phial which is really laudanum for the opium-eater, the "eldritch laugh," the vendetta of Mananaan, the unveiled mystery, the lonely house by the graveyard.

The seventh stage (405–15) represents Modern English of the nineteenth century. The profuseness of imagery and sentiment, the extravagance of diction, the varied subject matter—these are the traits of romantic style that Joyce uses to characterize the era. They might represent hundreds of writers of the time, yet it is easy to see that Joyce has settled on a few of the best-known writers because the very nature of the romantic writing demands an individuality that lends itself to parody. Leopold recalling the vivid picture of himself as a youth seems to be right out of Charles Lamb. The colorful language of De Quincey's opium dreams (and of Coleridge's poetry) is reflected in Bloom's meditations on the passage of time: "Elk and yak, the bulls of Bashan and of Babylon, mammoth and mastodon, they come trooping to the sunken sea, *Lacus Mortis*." The Greek revival, especially as seen in Landor, is easily recognized by the use of Greek names and a rather pompous style in the amusing account of Lenehan's luckless betting in the horse race that day. There is an excellent burlesque of the stately balanced periods of Macauley in the account of the debaters seated around the table, for example, the description of Bloom: "that vigilant wanderer, soiled by the dust of travel and combat and stained by the mire of an indelible dishonour, but from whose steadfast and constant heart no lure or peril or threat or degradation could ever efface the image of that voluptuous loveliness which the inspired pencil of Lafayette has limned for ages yet to come."[2]

The debate proceeds to scientific subjects, discussed in the language of the voluminous scientific writing inspired by the new discoveries of the age. While this passage might be taken as a parody of Darwin or Huxley, it is more properly leveled at numerous other scientists whose language was less skillful. The long passage wanders into chaotic sentences full of minutiae and much scientific jargon. Following this passage, the announcement of a "happy accouchement" leads to a delightful burlesque of sentimental fiction obviously aimed at Dickens though applicable to others: "Reverently look at her as she reclines there with the motherlight in her eyes, that longing hunger for baby fingers (a pretty sight it is to see), in the first bloom of her new motherhood, breathing a silent prayer of thanksgiving to One above, the Universal Husband."[3]

Three paragraphs follow of smooth diction and serious tone that might have been written by Newman, Ruskin, or Pater. Action breaks as the assembled youths burst out of doors on the way to Burke's tavern, but before they leave, a few deep breaths of fresh night air inspire an enthusiastic peroration in the best

[2] Joyce, *Ulysses*, 410.   [3] *Ibid.*, 413

evangelistic manner of Carlyle in *Sartor Resartus,* the high-flown English exclamations spotted at times with German and Latin. It is fitting that the nineteenth-century language should come to a climax in such a magnificent parody: "Thou sawest thy America, thy lifetask, and didst charge to cover like the transpontine bison. How saith Zarathusthra? Deine Kuh Truebsal melkest Du."[4]

The final stage (417–21) is the disintegration of English under the impact of twentieth-century slang and foreign contamination. Realistically, the last few episodes describe just what a group of inebriated intellectuals might say as they change drinking spots late at night. Tags of learned phrases mingle with incoherent nonsense, old jokes and popular sayings, church Latin and pig Latin, parodies of prayers, echoes of children's rimes and schoolboy talk, phrases from French, German, and Spanish, and imitation of various dialects (Chinese, Scotch, Jewish, Negro, French, and the peculiar speech of at least two regions of England). The whole scene is hilariously comical, though occasionally a serious note intrudes with amazing conciseness, as in the following comments on Joyce's common theme of England's military tyranny, especially over Ireland: "Tention. Proceed to the nearest canteen and there annex liquor stores. March! Tramp, tramp, tramp the boys are (attitudes!) parching. Beer, beef, business, bibles, bulldogs, battleships, buggery and bishops. Whether on the scaffold high. Beerbeef trample the bibles. When for Irelandear. Trample the trampellers. Thunderation! Keep the durned millingtary step. We fall. Bishops' boosebox. Halt!"[5]

The quick tempo accelerates, except for a few pauses to

[4] *Ibid.,* 416.
[5] *Ibid.,* 417.

vomit, to a sidesplitting parody of evangelistic, come-to-Jesus oratory.

And so the master of the English language has pictured his medium as developing from formless confusion to nobility of expression, yet ending in the obscurity of disintegration that results from trying to serve too many purposes. This is the historical picture of style, serving its purpose in *Ulysses* as a medium for the ingenious talk of drunken young intellectuals. The conventional language has deteriorated, leaving incoherence in its place. Joyce is concerned with his medium, however, and he will not let it rest here. To make any progress, he seems to say, we must try a new experiment away from the traditional. It may take many years for the work in progress to become *Finnegans Wake*. We must be patient and wait.

"Circe" (*episode 15*)

A detailed analysis of the 171 pages of printed text of this episode would be out of proportion in this book, yet a good idea of the technique and comic richness can be had from a summary of the many rapidly changing scenes that take place in the short time between Bloom's first pause before Bella Cohen's brothel and his entrance with Zoe Higgins. The first part, in which Bloom's thoughts on the events of his life are dramatized in scenes based on the past day, occupies thirty-five pages. The second part, enacting his glorious political rise and the equally rapid decline of his fortunes, fill nineteen more pages. The reader must bear in mind, however, that the following summary only suggests the main ideas and therefore gives few of the numerous minor associations that lend to the whole picture of Bloom's innermost nature an incredible richness.

Bloom pauses in the street before entering the brothel to which he has followed Stephen, and in the short time that he stands there many fantastic scenes created in his mind are projected into being and merge magically and swiftly into one another. First, his father appears like an elder in Zion, and Bloom changes to a smartly dressed young man. Then his mother appears like a "pantomime dame" in old-fashioned dress—crinoline, bustle, muttonleg sleeves, cameo brooch, and all.

After the vision of his father and mother, Bloom sees his wife in sensuous Oriental dress; he stammers and hides what he wants to say; she slaps his haunches and scolds him while a camel "lifting a foreleg, plucks from a tree a large mango fruit." Bloom is reminded of sticky lemon soap he carried in his pocket all day, and the vision of the soap rises in brightness to recite a couplet that Bloom might have used in one of his advertisements. There is still an air of playfulness when Gerty MacDowell, whom Bloom had seduced in his imagination that evening on the beach, is accused by a bawd of being a cheat. Gerty gives way to Mrs. Breen, and Bloom's daydreams of his early love escapades with her are interrupted only by random reminiscences dramatized, as when two blackfaced minstrels sing a familiar song, "then, chuckling, chortling, trumming, twanging, they diddle diddle cakewalk dance away."

Left in the miserable surroundings of nighttown at midnight, Bloom feeds a dog with a pigsfoot he had bought, and the watch apprehends him for being a nuisance. The dog quickly changes breeds—retriever, wolfdog, mastiff, bulldog, spaniel, boarhound, greyhound—setting the rapid pace for fantastic changes about to come. Bloom gives his identity as a dental surgeon, cousin of an Egyptian pasha who owns half Austria, but the card falls out of his hat reading "Henry Flower," the name he had assumed for his secret correspondence with Martha Clifford. Bloom tries to joke with the watch and explain the discrepancy, but Martha accuses him of breach of promise in the style of an old melodrama: "I'll tell my brother, the Bective rugger fullback, on you, heartless flirt."

Bloom defends himself before an imaginary jury, proclaiming the heroism of his father-in-law ("a most distinguished commander, a gallant upstanding gentleman, what do you call him, Majorgeneral Brian Tweedy"), the patriotism of his father, and his own service "with the colours for King and country" in the Boer War. Bloom gives his occupation as author-journalist, and immediately Myles Crawford, journalist from the "Aeolus" episode, appears at the telephone, quill in teeth, scarlet beak blazing, straw hat on head, and Spanish onions in one hand, protesting angrily. Philip Beaufoy, a sentimental novelist whose work Bloom has planned to imitate, then appears in accurate morning dress to accuse him of plagiarism of "the Beaufoy books of love and great possessions" which "are a household word throughout the kingdom." Bloom tries to protest, but Beaufoy goes on to accuse him of leading a "quadruple existence." A servant girl appears as a witness against Bloom and accuses him of molesting her. He tries to defend himself before the court, but the avalanche of sentimentality is so incoherent that it cannot be given verbatim. He excuses himself by saying he was a seven months' child nurtured by an aged, bedridden parent. He has erred, but now he wants "to lead a homely life in the evening of his days, permeated by the affectionate surroundings of the heaving bosom of his family." He says he wants to imitate the quiet household he once saw as he stood in the rain and looked in at the domestic peace, at innocent children lisping prayers, studying, playing the piano, "reciting the family rosary round the crackling Yulelog while in the boreens and green lanes the colleens with their swains strolled what times the strains of the organtoned melodeon Britannia metalbound with four acting stops and twelvefold bellows, a sacrifice, greatest bargain ever . . ."

From sentiment the cross-examination by contrast shifts to the sordid details of Bloom having once relieved himself in a plasterer's bucket, and Bloom appears "in a torn frock coat stained with whitewash, dinged silk hat sideways on his head, a strip of sticking plaster across his nose." Mr. J. J. O'Molloy then defends Bloom in eloquent oratory, pleading various extenuating circumstances, foreign extraction, heredity, the innate gentleness of the client, and finally hard luck through mortgaging of extensive properties at Agendath Netaim in faraway Asia Minor. O'Molloy, coughing blood, in his final plea pulls all the stops, paraphrasing a bit of oratory he had quoted that morning in the newspaper office: "When the angel's book comes to be opened if aught that the pensive bosom has inaugurated of soul transfigured and of soul transfiguring deserves to live I say accord the prisoner at the bar the sacred benefit of the doubt."

Bloom, in court dress now, gives as references the queens of Dublin society, whereupon three of the society ladies rise to accuse him of attempted seduction. First, Mrs. Yelverton Barry, "in lowcorsaged opal balldress and elbowlength ivory gloves, wearing a sabletrimmed brick quilted dolman, a comb of brilliants and panache of osprey in her hair," said Bloom had written her an anonymous letter making lewd suggestions on the basis of having seen her "peerless globes" as she sat below him in a theater. Next, Mrs. Bellingham, wrapped up to the nose in furs, "steps out of her brougham and scans through tortoiseshell quizzing-glasses which she takes from inside her huge opossum muff." As she proceeds with her accusations, however, she takes great pains to describe to the court her own charms and the armorial bearings of the Bellingham escutcheon. Finally, "the Honourable Mrs. Mervyn Talboys, in amazon costume, hard hat, jackboots cockspurred, vermilion waistcoat, fawn musketeer gauntlets with braided drums, long train held up and hunting crop with which she strikes her welt constantly," accuses Bloom of sending her obscene photographs and begging her to punish him, "to bestride and ride him, to give him a most vicious horsewhipping."

The uproarious scene that follows fades into reminiscences of other sexual experiences of the day, all products of his imagination, and then to the sentence of hanging. In his distress Bloom points out that the bomb with a time fuse, which the watch suspects him of having planted in the corner, is really a package of pig's feet and that he has been at a funeral. Immediately the dog, now a beagle with a dachshund coat, grows to human size and shape and takes on the gruesome and mutilated face of Paddy Dignam, who was buried that day. The grim humor of the scene is played up to the full. Paddy bays lugubriously and mocks the ghost of Hamlet's father, begs his listeners to keep his wife off that bottle of sherry, and looks for a lamppost to satisfy an animal need after drinking the quart of buttermilk that had been requested when his ghost appeared to the men in Kiernan's saloon during the afternoon.[6] The cemetery caretaker and the chaplain who buried him try to get Paddy back where he belongs, Father Coffey sleepy and hoarsely chanting "Jacobs Vobiscuits," and John O'Connell shouting for Paddy through a megaphone. Paddy wriggles forward, places an ear to the ground like the dog in the old Victor phonograph advertisements, and then says, "My master's voice!" (Incidentally, the reference here to the phonograph humorously mentioned in the "Hades" episode is even clearer when it is remembered that in England and on the continent "His Master's Voice" was not only the legal name for Victrola but a household synonym for all phonographs.) Paddy worms down through a coalhole, and "after him toddles an obese grandfather rat." As if Paddy were a fox gone to earth, Tom Rochford in hunting costume starts after him and is engulfed in the coalhole, much as he was in real life when he went to rescue someone fallen into a manhole.[7] On the columns of Rochford's new invention two discs "wobble eyes of nought" and the whole scene recedes, leaving Bloom talking to Zoe again outside the lighted whore house.

The great political rise and fall of Bloom the reformer is dramatized in nineteen pages (469–88) of vivid scenes. An interlude of salacious humor appears in the next conversation between Zoe and Bloom, such as the kisses twittering, warbling, cooing, "Icky licky micky sticky for Leo!" and Zoe mistaking the potato in Bloom's pocket for a hard chancre. But the fast moving scenes rich with comedy begin with Zoe's suggestion that Bloom make a stump speech about the evils of tobacco.

[6] *Ibid.*, 296.
[7] *Ibid.*, 227.

Bloom begins in workman's overalls and black jersey with red floating tie and apache cap, but after the chimes imitate the tale of Dick Whittington with their "Turn again, Leopold! Lord Mayor of Dublin!" we see him in alderman's gown and chain recommending public works. A torchlight procession brings in the Lord Mayor who moves that Bloom's speech be printed at public expense, and without a vote Councillor Sherlock announces it is carried unanimously. Bloom continues with impassioned oratory against "hideous hobgoblins produced by a horde of capitalistic lusts upon our prostituted labour." Almost instantly the city becomes decorated with festal splendor. A pillar of cloud suggests the analogy with Moses leading the children of Israel out of bondage, and a fife and drum band playing the "*Kol Nidre*" emphasizes the similarity. A grand procession in medieval splendor moves through the streets as the ladies from their balconies throw down rose petals on Bloom riding on a milk-white horse richly caparisoned, dressed in imperial robes. The procession is described in the manner of Rabelais: headed by the potentates of church and state, and followed by leaders of all religious sects as well as by thirty-five very odd kinds of tradesmen, such as lard refiners, ticket writers, riddle makers, and egg and potato factors.

Bloom is honored on all sides, even by a sunburst in the northwest, and is crowned as Leopold the First, "emperor president and king chairman, the most serene and potent and very puissant ruler of this realm." Bloom presumptuously nominates his horse, Capula Felix, as Grand Vizier and takes the princess Selene as his new queen. He is given the keys of Dublin and publicly shows that he is patriotically wearing green socks. He proudly reminds the people of their military glory in a speech that sounds like a mixture of Tennyson's "Charge of the Light Brigade" and a new crusade against the Saracens. He proclaims a new era and a new golden city, "the new Bloomusalem in the Nova Hibernia of the future." The construction of the new Bloomusalem begins, much like Napoleon's rebuilding of Paris and Mussolini's monumental changes in Rome, a colossal edifice of 40,000 rooms shaped like a huge pork kidney. In the process of construction, several buildings and monuments are demolished, numerous houses torn down, and the displaced inhabitants lodged in barrels and boxes marked in red with the letters "L. B."

The mysterious man in the mackintosh, whose identity had worried Bloom at Dignam's funeral, now springs up suddenly, accuses Bloom of being an impostor, and disappears. Meanwhile, Bloom rules like a benevolent despot, and the account of his acts reads like a very humorous satire of the ways of dictators and professional politicians. He gets rid of his enemies, such as members of standing committees. He doles out all kinds of gifts to the people, including commemoration medals, loaves and fishes, temperance badges, cigars, soupbones, candy, ready-made suits, forty days' indulgences, spurious coins, and "cheap reprints of the World's Twelve Worst books," all carefully itemized in Rabelais' style. He then tries to be all things to all men: shakes hands with a blind man, puts his arms around an old couple, enters into games with ragged children, plays with twin babies and talks baby talk to them, performs magician's tricks, consoles a widow, dances the Highland fling with grotesque antics, kisses the bedsores of a palsied veteran, trips up a fat policeman, teases a waitress playfully, eats a raw turnip offered by a farmer, refuses to accept a three-shilling debt offered by Hynes though he has been thinking of it all day, gives his coat to a beggar, and takes part in a stomach race with elderly cripples.

Bloom holds a court of conscience, where, like Sancho Panza, he seems to judge wisely and fairly; however, his reforms are too extensive and his views too liberal to suit all. It is perhaps all right to stand for "union of all, jew, moslem and gentile," for three acres with a cow for all children of nature, for saloon motor hearses, for compulsory manual labor for all, for electric dishwashers, for abolition of tuberculosis, lunacy, war, and mendicancy, and even for general amnesty and bonuses for all, but when he advocates "free money, free love, and a free lay church in a free lay state,"[8] Father Farley proclaims him "an episcopalian, an agnostic, an anythingarian to overthrow our holy faith," and others join in crying him down. Many enthusiastic women still look on him as their hero god and commit suicide in twelve different ways, including leaping from Nelson's Pillar into the great vat of Guinness's brewery and hanging themselves in stylish garters. But the attack grows and he is accused of being a stage Irishman, a plagiarist, a pagan debaucher, and finally a womanly man. After examination by Dr. Mulligan it is proclaimed that Bloom is about to have a baby, and a collection is taken up in the street for him, including blank checks, I.O.U.'s, and wedding rings. He gives birth to eight male yellow and white children, all handsome, "with valuable metallic faces, well made, respectably dressed and well conducted, speaking five modern languages fluently and interested in various arts and sciences."

Bloom finally plays out the role of Messiah in a sort of parody of Christ's Crucifixion. He is called upon for a miracle, such as

[8] *Ibid.*, 480.

prophesying the winner of a horse race. Instead, he does several parlor tricks, eats twelve dozen oysters (shells included), and makes his face resemble fourteen historical personages as different as Lord Beaconsfield, Lord Byron, and Robinson Crusoe. The Papal Nuncio then proclaims Bloom's genealogy in the manner of Christ's in the Gospel of St. Matthew, reflecting the analogy with the Messiah and the change of names of the wandering Jew over many generations. As if submitting to his crucifixion, Bloom seats himself in the pillory and "soft pantomime stones" are cast at him. He is set afire but rises phoenix-like from the flames. The daughters of Erin pray for him in a mock litany, and a choir of six hundred voices sings the "Allelulia Chorus." Thus ends the apocalypse of Messiah Bloom, and he lapses into a resigned state of acceptance that contemplates suicide in the language of a peasant right out of the Irish renaissance by way of a play of John M. Synge.

CHAPTER SEVEN

THE LITERARY ACHIEVEMENT OF

Ulysses

The common reader now has the tools for understanding *Ulysses* and for evaluating it as a piece of literature. The novel represents the resolving of Joyce's lifelong concern with matter and style, the happy combination of his attempt to express the universal in terms of the particular and his desire to enlarge the English language. Joyce pursued the quest still further in *Finnegans Wake* but with such daring experimentation in style that the ordinary reader is unwilling to follow him. *Ulysses* remains the high point of Joyce's literary career, a mixture of sound and sense, with such an enduring quality that critics rank it among the modern literary masterpieces. The measure of this enduring quality must be in terms of critical evaluation of matter and style.

First, in regard to matter, *Ulysses* is universal in its breadth and in the variety of subjects treated. There are few phases of modern life, conscious or subconscious, that are not touched upon in the book. That which affects most people—love, death, marriage, family, religion, business, pleasure—is repeated, varied, shifted, treated in many ways. Dozens of trades and professions are represented, from the gravedigger to the editor, and Bloom, solicitor of advertisements, touches them all sooner or later. All ranks of society from the whores of Nighttown to the Viceroy are in *Ulysses*, and Bloom associates with high and low alike. The scenes in Dublin are a grand slice of life, a cross-section of a busy modern city, symbolized by a funeral procession or a viceregal cortege crossing from one side to the other.

Morning, noon, afternoon, night—it is all there, the changing city in its many moods, the streets and trains and carriages full of people dominated by hope or despair, happiness or suffering. Perhaps the note of despair, or at least of futility, is dominant, because modern life is like that or Joyce makes us think so. At any rate, the slice of life is encyclopedic in the two hundred or so characters that Joyce brings to life on this Bloomsday of 1904.

Even the main characters complement each other. Leopold Bloom is earthy and practical, yet he is tolerant and peace loving. He is unwilling to stir up strife, yet bold enough to stand up for his principles against a prejudiced patriot or to risk danger to rescue the drunken Stephen late at night. Stephen Dedalus, on the other hand, is intellectual and impractical, overly sensitive to the love or dislike of others, very clever in speech and writing but seldom achieving anything by his cleverness. The two of them together would almost make one all-round man, but they both have one fault in common: they are both victims of the aggressive and extrovert Mulligans and Boylans. Only Molly Bloom with her charms and femininity can get the better of aggressive men like these, and she is completely without moral standards.

The three main characters together make a cross-section of humanity, but not one of them is noble, unless it be Bloom. Stephen is a priggish young intellectual, and I find it hard to sympathize with him, even when he is in trouble. I want to tell him to face up to Mulligan and give him back his taunts and teasing. Molly is not worth worrying about, but at least she knows what she wants and usually gets it.

Bloom is lovable, however, in spite of his weak and compromising moments. He has loved Molly and his father and his dead son, and nothing would please him more than to relive the old love with Molly and recapture the lost son in adopting Stephen as his spiritual son. In his most prosaic everyday moments he is something of a poet, wandering wide over the world in his imagination, feeling alike the ecstatic joys and the biting sorrows of mankind with a keen appetite. He is tolerant of everything except intolerance and prejudice, and he goes out of his way to relieve suffering or at least to show his sympathy. He meets with Martin Cunningham to help Patrick Dignam's widow, and he risks strange company at the maternity hospital to see that Mrs. Purefoy is safely delivered of her child. The poet in him never shows in his daily routine of prosaic advertising. Things are not what they seem, and Bloom risks martyrdom because his motives are mistaken or because he wishes to help a young man who for a moment replaces the son he had lost. And yet to the world the ridiculous Bloom is a comic figure. He becomes tragic only because we know his secret thoughts and desires.

The subject matter of *Ulysses* surely touches the universal even if it leaves the reader a little cold in his emotional reactions to Joyce's picture of the modern world. Joyce chose Ulysses as his all-round man, but it seems to be no accident that nearly every parallel between Joyce's story and Homer's is in reverse: Bloom is meek, compromising, and physically weak, while Ulysses was aggressive, bold, and strong; Molly is sensual and boastful of her lovers, while Penelope was the ancient model of marital fidelity.

It is as if Joyce were saying: here all of modern life is mirrored in the citizens of Dublin, but modern life is unheroic and filled with futility and despair. Surely we may agree that *Ulysses* is an encyclopedic picture of modern man but this universal subject matter is not its greatest ingredient. We must go to its style for that.

In style, Joyce is a master of the English language, a fabulous artificer in the medium of words even as the ancient Dedalus had been in mechanics. Few English writers since Shakespeare have been as fascinated as Joyce by the exciting quality of words. This desire to experiment with language, accentuated by the fact that he was an Irishman and aware of the alien tongue, showed itself early in his writing. As we have already seen, he depicts several times in his *Portrait of the Artist* the young writer's elation over the magic of words in creating literature, but never more vividly than in the surge of spirits when Stephen decided to devote himself to writing instead of the priesthood, when turning seaward

he drew forth a phrase from his treasure and spoke it softly to himself: A day of dappled seaborne clouds. The phrase and the day and the scene harmonised in a chord. Words. Was it their colours? He allowed them to glow and fade, hue after hue: sunrise gold, the russet and green of apple orchards, azure of waves, the greyfringed fleece of clouds. No, it was not their colours: it was the poise and balance of the period itself. Did he then love the rhythmic rise and fall of words better than their associations of legend and colour? Or was it that, being as weak of sight as he was shy of mind, he drew less pleasure from the reflection of the glowing sensible world through the prism of a language many coloured and richly storied than from the contemplation of an inner world of individual emotions mirrored perfectly in a lucid supple periodic prose.[1]

In this passage there is the prophecy of Joyce's concern with the stream of consciousness. This high purpose, so ably portrayed later in *Ulysses*, could only be made effective, Joyce felt, by making over the medium of the writer, by injecting something new into language that would peel the old husks from words and make them glow with new association. Stephen Dedalus, having made his decision, reflects upon the casual words he meets in the street, feeling "that they had been so silently emptied of instantaneous sense until every mean shop legend bound his mind like the words of a spell and his soul shrivelled up sighing with age as he walked on in a lane among heaps of dead language."[2]

This interest in language and concern with words, so vividly portrayed in the early work, reached their highest artistic effect, I believe, in *Ulysses*. It is futile, of course, to try to separate the style of *Ulysses* from the story of Leopold and Molly Bloom, of Stephen Dedalus and other citizens of Dublin. The odyssey of modern man is the warp of the finished cloth. The language, the style, the words called up to fit the mood of each individual episode—these are the woof, the threads that could not stand alone but nevertheless add the colors to make the finished pattern. Together they make the picture of modern life, yet if I had to choose the more vigorous of the two qualities of *Ulysses*, style or development of theme, I should take style as the more exciting

[1] 194.
[2] *Ibid.*, 208.

and the one likely to be of more permanent value. For Joyce's greatest gift is language, the ability to get the right word even if he has to invent it. He chooses to paint a mood and by magic it appears.

For example, notice how he builds up the sleepy, lotus-eating mood evoked by the sight of choice blends of tea in a shop window:

> The far east. Lovely spot it must be: the garden of the world, big lazy leaves to float about on, cactuses, flowery meads, snaky lianas they call them. Wonder is it like that. Those Cinghalese lobbing around in the sun, in *dolce far niente*. Not doing a hand's turn all day. Sleep six months out of twelve. Too hot to quarrel. Influence of the climate. Lethargy. Flowers of idleness. The air feeds most. Azotes. Hothouse in Botanic gardens. Sensitive plants. Waterlilies. Petals too tired to. Sleeping sickness in the air. Walk on roseleaves.[3]

Here Joyce begins with the extended metaphor of the earthly paradise in the poppy warmth of a southern climate. He reinforces the luxuriant growth of nature with the indolence of human beings, suggested by the lazy drowsiness of the Cinghalese and the favorite phrase, "It is sweet to do nothing," of the sun-loving Italians. The indolent mood then begins to affect the style itself, allowing the choppy phrases from Bloom's stream of consciousness to pile up metaphors describing plants that close their leaves at night, too tired to make the effort to open them. The climax of softness is reached in the suggestion of walking on rose leaves,

[3] Joyce, *Ulysses,* 70.

soft to the touch yet fragile; they will fade with the touch of feet yet become more fragrant in the act.

Joyce is equally skillful in creating moods that are ugly and even repulsive. In Burton's restaurant at noon, for example, Bloom is repelled by the sight of mass mastication, and the disgust of the reader is aroused in much the same way as was the pleasurable indolence of the east: "Perched on high stools by the bar, hats shoved back, at the tables calling for more bread no charge, swilling, wolfing gobfuls of sloppy food, their eyes bulging, wiping wetted moustaches. A pallid suetfaced young man polished his tumbler knife fork and spoon with his napkin. New set of microbes. A man with an infant's saucestained napkin tucked round him shovelled gurgling soup down his gullet. A man spitting back on his plate: halfmasticated gristle: no teeth to chewchewchew it."[4]

The word magic of Joyce in *Ulysses* thus serves contrasting moods in portraying both ugliness and beauty. In the past the great English poets have always been able to depict the ugly when the subject demanded it. Spenser painted foulness in the monster Error, Milton in Sin's progeny at the gates of Hell, Shakespeare in his many villains. Joyce has perhaps more than his share of the ugly to accentuate the despair of modern man, yet his picture, in the "Hades" episode, of death in all its phases would not be complete without this description of decaying corpses that fairly turns the reader's stomach: "I daresay the soil would be quite fat with corpse manure, bones, flesh, nails, charnelhouses. Dreadful. Turning green and pink, decomposing. Rot quick in damp earth. The lean old ones tougher. Then a kind of a tallowy kind of a

4 *Ibid.*, 166.

cheesy. Then begin to get black, treacle oozing out of them. Then dried up. Deathmoths. Of course the cells or whatever they are go on living. Changing about. Live for ever practically. Nothing to feed on feed on themselves."[5]

It seems clear that Joyce used words masterfully to portray beauty and ugliness, tragedy and comedy, despair and joy, as the demand of the moment dictated. Naturally, any attempt to show this quality must be somewhat subjective. Yet the linguist can furnish the critic with some additional evidence by a few observations on Joyce's use of individual words in *Ulysses*. We must recognize at the outset that such a study has only a limited value, for as in speech the words cannot be torn from their context without losing that association value which constitutes their true meaning. An individual word is of chief interest to the etymologist alone, who by tracing its complete history can add much to our knowledge of the ways of language. If one must isolate the word from its context, however, perhaps the best approach is to view the picture as a whole. This has been made possible for our purpose by a *Word Index to Ulysses* compiled in 1937 at the University of Wisconsin under the direction of Professor Miles Hanley.

Aside from its usefulness in tracing the recurrent images and associations, this index also throws some interesting light on Joyce's use of words. Of 29,899 different words used in *Ulysses*, 16,432 occur only once, but a study of these will show that they are usually quite easily understood in the context. For example, let us take the first uncapitalized word in each column under H in the *Word Index*. Less than one-third of these words show any

[5] *Ibid.*, 107.

appreciable disagreement with the word frequency of the 20,000 words most commonly found in college reading.[6] Only four words are not in this list, and they are easily explained: *heresiarch* is a theme word involved in Stephen's rejection of the Church, and *hest, hig,* and *hugebearded* occur, for obvious reasons, only once in *Ulysses. Hest* is uttered by a boy being hanged; because his "tongue protrudes violently,"[7] his speech is distorted. *Hig* is part of a children's rhyme: "You hig, you hog, you dirty dog."[8]

Hugebearded is one of those expressive compounds that occur so frequently as to be a characteristic of Joyce's style. It occurs in a passage that contains a number of them: "Ben Jumbo Dollard, rubicund, musclebound, hairynostrilled, hugebearded, cabbageeared, shaggychested, shockmaned, fatpapped, stands forth, his loins and genitals tightened into a pair of black bathing bagslops."[9] Many such compounds appear commonly enough in literary English and profusely in colloquial English, but a surprising number of the compounds in *Ulysses* are Joyce's own invention. Time after time they are used with a combined freshness and aptness that make them poetical. Professor George P. Krapp, one of the first linguists to recognize Joyce's uncanny skill with words, noted such effective compounds as "jet beads . . . inkshining in the sun"[10] and "he watched through peacocktwittering lashes the southing sun."[11] Here are a few more: green and gold *beaconjars* in a chemist's shop;[12] the gravedigger's spade *blueglancing;*[13] fists

[6] Edward L. Thorndike, *Teacher's Word Book* (New York, Columbia University Press, 1931).

[7] Joyce, *Ulysses,* 578.

[8] *Ibid.,* 486.   [11] *Ibid.,* 50.

[9] *Ibid.,* 510.   [12] *Ibid.,* 82.

[10] *Ibid.,* 216   [13] *Ibid.,* 111.

bigdrumming on padded knees;[14] lonely Shakespeare is *Christfox*;[15] two urchins eating suckers have *yellowslobbered* mouths;[16] followers of Plato *creepycrawl* after Blake's buttocks;[17] and in an orchestra brasses are like asses braying through *uptrunks*.[18]

Joyce never uses a hyphen to spell his compounds, and so even ordinary compounds may appear odd, but this very feeling for the compactness of words has led him to invent numerous new words from old ones. The use of compounds was common in Homer and a characteristic device of early Germanic poetry. Joyce has revived the kennings of *Beowulf* and Old Norse poetry with striking effectiveness.

Similar tests made by random checks of controlled samples from the *Word Index* and compared with other frequency lists show roughly the same result, that Joyce's reputation for unintelligibility is not justified by his use of individual words in *Ulysses*. At least two-thirds of the words in *Ulysses* are found with the same frequency as those in the ordinary reading of the educated adult. Recent studies in the style of other authors show that about the same proportion appears in most contemporary literature.[19] Even those words in *Ulysses* which appear infrequently elsewhere are not usually hard to understand when taken in their context. Furthermore, an examination of the words that appear only once in *Ulysses* shows that most of them are vivid Joycean compounds, strange spelling of sounds, or fragments of words chopped off in the course of rushing thoughts and rem-

[14] *Ibid.*, 140. [16] *Ibid.*, 222. [18] *Ibid.*, 280.
[15] *Ibid.*, 191. [17] *Ibid.*, 184.
[19] George A. Miller, *Language and Communication* (New York, McGraw-Hill, 1951), 88–92; G. U. Yule, *The Statistical Study of Literary Vocabulary* (Cambridge, Cambridge University Press, 1944).

iniscences. Others are learned or rare words deliberately used to call up a mood or set the flavor for a passage, whether legal, scientific, or literary, scholarly or popular, archaic or invented for the purpose.

Clearly then, Joyce is experimenting in *Ulysses* with changes in regular words, but he has not yet gone to wholesale invention of new words. *Ulysses* in this respect is but the prelude to *Finnegans Wake*, for in the earlier work Joyce is content to stretch the English language by stylistic devices rather than by tampering with individual words. The difficulty lies not in word recognition but in the rapid shift in associated ideas on the one hand and in a tremendous body of allusions, mostly literary, on the other hand. The association of ideas is the very heart of Joyce's fictional technique and is used throughout *Ulysses*. The use of literary allusions, especially in the imitation of older literature to set the tone of a passage, is common enough in *Ulysses* and even dominates the episodes in the newspaper office, at the library, and in the maternity hospital. Too often the critic has admired Joyce's ingenuity, however, while deploring the result as a tour de force. Yet careful study shows that Joyce, the master of words, has molded his medium to suit his purpose. If his enthusiasm for words occasionally gets the upper hand over the novelist, we can excuse the nodding in our admiration of his technical skill.

Next to the word magic that shows itself in mastery of style, the quality in *Ulysses* that seems most powerful, and often least appreciated, is the comic satire. Joyce's resemblance to Rabelais, already seen in my study of the "Cyclops" episode, appears throughout the book in the spirit of ribald humor that reaches a climax in the "Circe" episode. Joyce is indeed much like a twentieth-century Rabelais who wishes to laugh away the complex futility of modern life with its technological efficiency and its moral immaturity. He pursues this serious satiric purpose with the same insatiable love of words and the same hearty disdain of puritanical squeamishness that Rabelais had. He pursues it, too, with the same avowed intent that Swift had when he wrote A *Tale of a Tub* and the first two books of *Gulliver's Travels*, that of laughing men out of their follies and vices instead of lashing them in the manner of Juvenal.

In *Ulysses*, Joyce is indeed in the same great tradition of comic satire that we find in Rabelais and Swift—and in Cervantes, too, for the great Spaniard began his comedy with the idea of ridiculing the follies of medieval chivalry and ended by creating the tragicomic characters of Don Quixote and Sancho Panza. Joyce's comic powers have been neglected by most critics[20] because *Ulysses* contains so much besides, combining tears and laughter as it attempts to achieve encyclopedic universality. For example, the book begins with the deadly seriousness of Stephen, who in his lighter moments contributes a sort of ponderous humor in his intellectual play on words, and it ends with the earthy and frivolous seriousness of Molly, whose playfulness is displayed more readily in sexual encounters than in comedy. But there is still enough comedy in *Ulysses* to place it in the great tradition of

[20] Tributes to Joyce's comic powers appeared in two recent pieces of critical cims after I had written my version of the subject. Sol Stein, *University of Kansas City Review*, XVIII (1952), 241–54, says that *Ulysses* is great comedy to be taken seriously but not somberly. Arland Ussher, *Three Great Irishmen: Shaw, Yeats, Joyce* (New York, Devinadair, 1943), 119, calls Joyce "a great humorous writer." Eugene Sheehy in his reminiscences of schooldays with Joyce (*May it please the Court*, Dublin, 1951), gives many instances of Joyce's comic ability as a boy.

comic satire. Over and over again we see this quality in the realistic banter of carefree Irishmen at play, in the numerous scenes of incidental satire, and in the tragicomic figure of Leopold Bloom himself.[21]

The fact that Joyce is a master of the comic spirit who loves his jokes does not mean that he did not treat *Ulysses* seriously as a work of art. I get a bit impatient at those "friends" of Joyce who pretend to let us in on the great secret that he was in the habit of deliberately bamboozling a credulous public. In the case of Mrs. Mary Colum, who said that Joyce was playing a joke when he pretended to borrow his stream-of-consciousness technique from Dujardin's obscure novel, it does not matter much. When Oliver St. John Gogarty tells the world in confidence, however, that *Ulysses* is a gigantic hoax, the game has gone too far. Some credulous person who has not read Joyce may take Gogarty seriously.[22]

Ulysses is a highly comical book with a serious purpose, like *Gulliver's Travels* and *Gargantua and Pantagruel*. The tone of this comic seriousness is set by the character of Leopold Bloom, the chief figure in the book. From beginning to end Bloom is a tragicomic figure of the ridiculous little man who dreams but dares not assert himself unless he is pushed to the wall, a combination of Walter Mitty and J. Alfred Prufrock. Even Bloom excites laughter in various ways as the day progresses. In the morn-

[21] The title of "*Ulysses*, jokebook of the giants," used by Josef Baake ("Das Riesenscherzbuch Ulysses," *Bonner Studien zur englischen Philolgie*, Vol. XXXII, 1937, 1–101) is misleading, yet the study contains excellent detailed analysis of Joyce's satire in *Ulysses* on the esoteric mysticism of the Irish Renaissance (32–48) and on Shakespearean discussion (72–97) as well as studies of other themes.

[22] Ussher, *Three Great Irishmen*, nevertheless says he can sympathize with those who make such crude arguments "more than with that earnest sect for whom the world began on June 16th 1904 in the Holles St. Hospital," 119.

ing he dreams and is not yet frustrated; from noon to midnight he meets the cruel world that laughs as he squirms; late at night he is weary from his buffeting by the world, resigned and slightly triumphant in his compromising way, more to be pitied than ridiculed. And so the last word is the serious one with Bloom, as it was with Don Quixote before him.

When Bloom first enters the book in the fourth episode ("Calypso") of *Ulysses*, the tone of the writing lightens and becomes cheerful. The young Joyce was too serious in his writing about Stephen Dedalus to do much joking, and so the only humor in *Portrait of the Artist* and in the continuation of Stephen in the first part of *Ulysses* is of the heavy-handed sort. Where comedy does appear, it is in the mouths of Stephen's comrades, as in the banter of the university students in *Portrait of the Artist* and in the relentless ridicule of the arrogant Buck Mulligan in the first episode ("Telemachus") of *Ulysses*. For example, Mulligan blasphemes the Christian church, parodies the Mass, changes Homer's wine-dark sea to "snotgreen," and sings a scurrilous ballad ridiculing the virgin birth. No one is inclined to laugh, however, except the speakers themselves.

Then Bloom enters the scene, and immediately the reader begins to smile sympathetically with the genial pictures of the homely Irish Jew talking to the cat and putting his talisman potato in his pocket. Bloom paints a ridiculous picture of his father-in-law ("old Tweedy's big moustaches leaning on a long kind of a spear") in his idyllic Oriental dream. He muses on his daughter Milly's childish escapades and, while sitting on the toilet, contemplates writing a sentimental story.

The genial mood continues with Bloom's walk through the

streets after breakfast, meditating upon the ways in which he can escape from the troubled everyday world. He tears up the love letter of his secret correspondent and muses on how a man could as easily tear up a check for a million pounds, the profit from fifteen million gallons of porter. He rejects religion but not before he has seen the amusing side of missions to China or to Africa, where he pictures cannibals entranced by a missionary's spectacles flashing in the sun, "sitting round in a ring with blub lips, entranced."

The episode of Dignam's funeral ("Hades"), with its serious overtones of death, contains some priceless gems of grim humor. Sentimental death notices in the paper are pathetic but laughable, especially the verses beginning "It is now a month since dear Henry fled To his home above in the sky." A story of a coffin upset on the road brings up the ridiculous possibility of Dignam's corpse "rolling over stiff in the dust in a brown habit too large for him." The funeral service introduces a grim picture of resurrection tied in with a blasphemous pun: "That last day idea. Knocking them all up out of their graves. Come forth, Lazarus! And he came fifth and lost the job. Get up! Last day! Then every fellow mousing around for his liver and his lights and the rest of his traps. Find damn all of himself that morning."[23]

The joking becomes more and more grim as Bloom's thoughts go to ghosts and decomposition. He figures the dead would like to hear an odd joke: "You must laugh sometimes so better do it that way. Gravediggers in *Hamlet*. Shows the profound knowledge of the human heart."[24] Reflections on immor-

[23] Joyce, *Ulysses*, 104.
[24] *Ibid.*, 107.

tality take a humorous twist with the gramophone used to recall poor old greatgrandfather after dinner on a Sunday: "Kraahraark! Hellohellohello amawfullyglad kraark awfullygladaseeragain hellohello amarawf kopthsth."[25] The episode is full of serious reflections on death and many related ideas, but the comedy is as much a part of it as it was of the Irish ballad, "Finnegan's Wake."

From the middle of the afternoon Bloom becomes more serious, while the comedy of the outside world becomes more uproarious and the satire on the world's folly and pretense becomes sharper. The change seems to come in the Ormond bar ("Sirens") where the mood is dominantly gay and playful to contrast with the somber mood of Bloom, meditating on marital infidelity. The episode is filled with incidental satire on music, and the very atmosphere of the place is lighthearted as the two young barmaids throw "young heads back, bronze gigglegold, to let freefly their laughter." The fugue on the words bronze, gold, laughter, and giggle gives way to the masculine banter of Dedalus and Lenehan, the conquering swagger of Blazes Boylan, the bulky slops of "barreltone" Ben Dollard, and the game of snapping the garters of the barmaids. Singing and joking, well suited to Dublin's male prowess parading its talents, fill the air until they become the symbol of Boylan's assignation with Molly, the gayest of accompaniments to Bloom's loneliness.

The gaiety and laughter of the "Sirens" episode is a prelude to the magnificent comedy that follows, for in this and the four succeeding episodes Joyce displays his richest comic repertory even while Bloom becomes more serious. In Kiernan's saloon ("Cyclops") the overwhelming parody of jargon and the intense

[25] *Ibid.*, 112.

satire on chauvinism and violence are but a foil to Bloom's tolerance and love of peace. In the interlude that takes place along the beach ("Nausicaa") the burlesque of erotic sentimentality in the first part of the episode contrasts violently with the loneliness and spent emotion of the second part. In the maternity hospital ("The Oxen of the Sun") the drunken banter of young intellectuals is a boisterous accompaniment to Bloom's solicitous anxiety over Stephen. Finally, the magic transformations of the brothel episode ("Circe") portray a bewildering comedy of human desires and bring out roaring laughter even while they lay bare the secret thoughts of all. Perhaps Mr. W. Y. Tindall is close to the truth when he concludes: "Like Shaw, Joyce was the most serious and most profound when at his gayest. His humor is the proof of understanding and the sign of equanimity."[26]

As the book progresses and Bloom becomes more serious, the comic accompaniment becomes more boisterous until it reaches a climax in the dramatized incongruities of the "Circe" episode. Meanwhile, satire on many phases of modern life is rich and varied throughout the book. Sometimes it is incidental to the main purpose, like the satire on music in the "Sirens" episode or the burlesque of a sentimental love story in the "Nausicaa" episode. Again, it becomes the main theme of an episode where the technique is specially designed to ridicule human folly, like the satire in "Aeolus" on rhetorical bombast of all kinds from newspaper headlines to eloquent oratory, or like the satire in "Scylla and Charybdis" on learning and the futility of scintillating criticism.

More often, however, Joyce's all-pervasive satire is part of

[26] *James Joyce: His Way of Interpreting the Modern World* (New York, Twentieth Century Library, 1950), 126.

the Irish setting for the universal picture of man. Irish blarney is not too different from wordiness and bombastic jargon in any other place, and so we can recognize our own Aeolian windiness in the wordplay at the newspaper office as well as in the Rabelaisian inflations at Kiernan's saloon where it is merely a part of a more serious theme. Irish nationalism, it is true, has been whetted to unusual sharpness by the aggravations of many years of English rule, but the hatred of the Sassenach by Irish patriots in *Ulysses* reflects an exaggerated regionalism that makes us appreciate Joyce's universal satire on the professional patriot in other countries. The Irish church, especially the Jesuit Society, receives particular attention from Joyce because of his education in Jesuit schools and his later rejection of the Church, but back of the personal criticism is the larger comment on established religion and its place in the modern world.

Along with satire on these important phases of modern life, many interesting smaller topics in *Ulysses* achieve a kind of universality. The choice of a half-Jew for his hero gives Joyce the opportunity to satirize the racial prejudices of Irishmen, who by their very circumstances should have been more tolerant. In his numerous satirical references to the cult of Hindu mysticism prevalent in Dublin in his youth, Joyce ridicules not only AE (George Russell) and other prominent Dubliners but also cultists and faddists in general. The fast-moving scenes of the "Circe" episode satirize hundreds of aspects of modern life from the vanity of "high society" ladies to the tricks of politicians.

The comic method of Joyce is best seen in the examples already cited profusely in my analysis of *Ulysses*. Incongruity is, of course, the very essence of the basic comedy: incongruity of character in Bloom himself, and incongruity of situation, especially in the "Sirens," "Cyclops," "Oxen of the Sun," "Circe," and "Eumaeus" episodes. Puns are used in plenty, not only for the incongruity of the two meanings but also for the multiple associations that Joyce later exploits in *Finnegans Wake*. Parody is a common device in *Ulysses*, more often in the form of a casual allusion to a famous quotation or title but also as a burlesque of a style of writing ("Sirens," "Nausicaa," "Eumaeus") or of a chronological period ("The Oxen of the Sun").

Any attempt to illustrate Joyce's humor by specific examples would require too much space, for the casual banter of Irishmen in lighthearted moods is realistically portrayed many times in *Ulysses* and other writings of Joyce. Take the "Aeolus" episode in the newspaper office, for example, and listen to Lenehan, O'Madden Burke, J. J. O'Molloy, Mulligan, Professor MacHugh, and Myles Crawford with their puns, jokes, limericks, and hilarious general foolery. A short sample is the comment on the resemblance of the British Empire to Rome:

> That's it, he said. We are the fat. You and I are the fat in the fire. We haven't got the chance of a snowball in hell.
>
> Wait a moment, professor MacHugh said, raising two quiet claws. We mustn't be led away by words, by sounds of words. We think of Rome, imperial, imperious, imperative.
>
> He extended elocutionary arms from frayed stained shirt cuffs, pausing:
>
> What was their civilisation? Vast, I allow: but vile. Cloacae: sewers. The Jews in the wilderness and in the mountaintop said: It is *meet to be here. Let us build an altar to*

Jehovah. The Roman, like the Englishman who follows in his footsteps, brought to every new shore on which he set his foot (on our shore he never set it) only his cloacal obsession. He gazed about him in his toga and he said: *It is meet to be here. Let us construct a watercloset.*

Which they accordingly did do, Lenehan said. Our old ancient ancestors, as we read in the first chapter of Guinness's, were partial to the running stream.

They were nature's gentlemen, J. J. O'Molloy murmured. But we have also Roman law.

And Pontius Pilate is its prophet, professor MacHugh responded.[27]

Or listen at Ormond's saloon to the barmaid sirens, Douce and Kennedy, as they dispense drinks and, laughing, inspire the gay talk and witty thoughts of Lenehan, Boylan, Ben Dollard, and Simon Dedalus. The joking and banter give way to satirical description of music, but Joyce shows meanwhile how he can reproduce Irish conversation as he did in *Dubliners* but use it now more playfully as part of the comic satire beating out its boisterous accompaniment to Bloom's loneliness. For example, Simon Dedalus jokes with the barmaid to set the tone of gay inanities:

That was exceedingly naughty of you, Mr. Dedalus told her and pressed her hand indulgently. Tempting poor simple males. Miss Douce of satin douced her arm away.

O go away, she said. You're very simple, I don't think. He was.

27 Joyce, *Ulysses,* 129.

Well now, I am, he mused. I looked so simple in the cradle they christened me simple Simon.[28]

Lenehan enters and describes Stephen to his father in mock-heroic vein: "The *elite* of Erin hung upon his lips. The ponderous pundit, Hugh MacHugh, Dublin's most brilliant scribe and editor and that minstrel boy of the wild wet west who is known by the euphonious appellation of the O'Madden Burke."[29]

Whether it is realistic conversation or fantastic dramatization of thoughts, the comedy is full-bodied and natural in *Ulysses*, even as it is secretive and artificial in *Finnegans Wake*. Comedy is the sign of Joyce's maturity—absent for the most part in the earlier works, it is the one distinctly new element that is added to the search for the picture of universal man and helps to make *Ulysses* an enduring book, for vigor of style with its inventiveness of language was already in the earlier works, at least in an incipient form.

We can now add together all the ingredients that make up *Ulysses:* universal subject matter, including the stream of consciousness that reveals all and yet sometimes bewilders with its conciseness; experimentation with new techniques that enlarge the possibilities of the English language; and the comic satire that lends maturity and sometimes hilarity to the matter. The result, in my opinion, is a work of enduring quality, a masterpiece of modern literature.

[28] *Ibid.*, 257.
[29] *Ibid.*, 258.

CHAPTER EIGHT

finnegans wake:
OR EVERYMAN IN DUBLIN

Not long after the publication of *Ulysses* in 1922, the literary world noted the first appearances in print of a new kind of work by Joyce. In 1925 portions of the new "Work in Progress" were printed in various periodicals, and, from then until the publication in 1939 of the completed book as *Finnegans Wake*, the literary world read the fragments with increasing curiosity and a mixture of admiration and awe. Critics began explaining the startling new style, and as early as 1929 an impressive group of contributors published a critical symposium on the book, *Our Exagmination Round his Factification for Incamination of Work in Progress*.

It was soon evident that Joyce had done it again. Those critics who thought that *Ulysses* was the last word in literary experiments had not considered Joyce's lifelong interest in words and his desire to push the bounds of his artistic medium farther and farther from the conventional. While some critics examined and admired and explained, others took up the old cry of unintelligibility, this time with more reason than in the case of *Ulysses*. Many admirers of *Ulysses* felt that Joyce had gone too far in this new work, and even the most serious critics have usually had some qualifications on *Finnegans Wake* as an artistic composition.

My only concern with Joyce's last book at this time is to show the ordinary reader that, artistically, *Finnegans Wake* is the logical culmination of the two qualities of Joyce's writing that interested me most in *Ulysses*, his mastery of words and his facility in comic satire. Taken in small doses, it can be fun even to the casual reader, provided he knows the rules of the game, and the casual reader, you may be sure, will never take it in more than small selections. I realize that Joyce's purpose is very serious, transcending time and place and individual characters, but I leave that phase of the work to the many good critics who have already written much and will continue to write more.

Most of the scorn directed at Joyce's inventiveness in language, it must in fairness be admitted, has been not at *Ulysses* but at these more recent experiments in *Finnegans Wake*. The proliferant multiplication of neologisms in that work is, to put it mildly, somewhat appalling. The style is so unusual that it has kept Joyce's disciples busy explaining the work; and while Dante's *Divine Comedy* was considered difficult enough to call forth at least eleven commentaries within eighty years of the author's death, Joyce's last book had the doubtful honor of having an "exagmination" in book form published ten years before the work itself, and a few years after publication (1944) a lengthy commentary ironically called *A Skeleton Key to Finnegans Wake*.

My "exagmination" is concerned only with the strange technique arising from the artist's concern with words and with the comedy that frequently results from the new inventions. Joyce has here pushed to an extreme, and sometimes to an absurdity, his youthful desire to make writing come nearer music. His very language has changed. He has given words a greater load to carry, blended them until they yield a harmony of meanings, analogous to the harmony of sounds in a musical chord. He has, in other words, tried to make language polyphonic rather than melodic in quality. The common reader may never read *Finnegans Wake* with any eagerness, but he will want to know what Joyce is trying to do and how he does it. This I shall try to explain briefly.

In its simplest form this strange-looking language is a coalescing of words to produce a set of semantic associations. The blending of two or more words into one is an ordinary linguistic device that has given rise to such common telescoped words as *crouch*, *squash*, and *splatter*, and to such jocular words as *alcoholiday*, *smog*, and *chortle*. Lewis Carrol used such blends for humor, *Time* magazine uses them for brevity and novelty, and advertisers use them every day for their trade names. In *Finnegans Wake*, Joyce uses the device constantly and with startling effect: the masters of a boys' school are *kinderwardens*; to berate with reverberating vituperation is to *viterberate*; going to heaven on an escalator is *celescalating*; and all the skyscraper associations of higher, hierarch, architectonic, tiptop, toploft, and lofty are blended in *hierarchitectitiptitoploftical*.

This use of blends is similar to the pun, a time-honored device that Joyce is bringing back into literature. For example, *acheseyeld* suggests not only the basic word exiled but also, either by spelling or sound, the words aches, acheseye for longing, eld for old age and perhaps German *ach* (an exclamation of dismay); *Mississliffi* suggests the Mississippi, the Liffey River in Dublin, and the female element in nature that the Liffey represents in the story; *funferal* by sight suggests funeral, by sound fun for all and fanfare, prominent elements in an Irish wake. These puns are carefully worked into the general idea of the particular passage, not thrown in for merriment, and yet a good vaudeville comedian could pick up some good ones for his repertory. For example, *roaratorio* is a blend of roar and oratorio, a good description of a noisy concert, and *cremoaning* fiddles a blend of the famous Cremona violins and the characteristic moan of subdued violin music. The critic is aware that this device is really a metaphor, a part of all authentic poetry, yet surely he may also enjoy the pure fun it offers.

In this blending of words and ideas the analogy to the musical chord is apparent; words are played in unison to produce a harmony of associated ideas. The next step is to extend this to phrases: over a framework of proverbs, famous quotations, snatches of old songs, slang, clichés, or anything familiar, Joyce weaves a new association of ideas by changing the familiar to something that sounds enough like the new idea to call up a whole set of desired associations in the reader's mind. *Shoutmost shoviality* (shout, shove) and *eatmost boviality* (eat, drink, bovine) are amusing variations of the cliché, "utmost joviality." *Fadograph of a yestern scene* builds on the phrase, "photograph of a western scene," a ludicrous suggestion of a picture dim with age. The French proverb that serves as motto for the English Order of the Garter, *"Honi soit qui mal y pense"* (Evil is to him who evil thinks) appears in the description of a flirt as "honeys wore camelia paints." Christ's words, "Thou art Peter, and on this rock I build my church" becomes *thuartpeatrick*, suggesting the special quality of the Irish church with peat and Patrick (and incidentally calling to mind the fact that Christ used puns).

In a jocular passage Joyce describes the effects of devastating passion in the language of an old-fashioned grammar like Lindley Murray's: "O love it is the commonknounest thing how it pashes the plutous and the paupe. Pop! And egg she active or spoon she passive, all them fine clauses in Lindley's and Murrey's never braught the participle of a present to a desponent hortatrixy, vindicatively I say it from her postconditional future. Lumpsome is who lumpsum pays. Quantity counts though accents falter."[1]

In a satirical description of a conventional English army officer, Joyce uses Sandhurst (England's West Point), *champaign* (map of battle), and *plankrieg* (mixed English and German for war plan): "this soldier-author-batman for all his commontoryism is just another of those souftseized bubbles [soft, South-Seas Bubble] who never quite got the sandhurst out of his eyes so that the champaign he draws for us is as flop as plankrieg."

The whole pattern of an episode may be further complicated by additional blends suggestive of the subject matter, or tone, of the whole. A passage on Wellington and Napoleon is filled with military terms and names of battles. Perhaps the best example, however, is the chapter printed separately as "Anna Livia Plurabelle," where the gossip of two Irish washerwomen blends with the more universal theme of the dualism of male and female, tree and river, and to these is added by means of puns the names of rivers and various geographical terms (I say added because they do not appear in the first version). For example, tiger's becomes *tigris*, ask us becomes *oxus*, the wind becomes *derwent*, and tell me is spelled to suggest the Greek astronomer and geographer Ptolemy.

A single passage must suffice for illustration of the effectiveness of this method in suggesting themes. This is near the beginning of the book, where Finnegan's trade of builder becomes mixed with the ancient Tower of Babel and with such modern

[1] Joyce, *Finnegans Wake*, 269.

skyscrapers as the Woolworth Building and the Eiffel Tower. The dreamer here takes on the significant name of Haroun Childeric Eggeberth, suggesting the mixed nationality of the child born of an egg. The overtones of the first part are the names of the books of the Bible describing the early history of the Hebrews. The allusion to Addison's Mohammedan, who sticks his head in a tub of water to allow an eternity of time to elapse, emphasizes the relativity of time. The reference to the dreamer's wife Annie fits in with the obvious phallic symbols of tall buildings and with the erotic connotations of *fondseed* (fancied), *undress*, and *caligulate* (calculate and the Roman emperor Caligula). The word *erigenating* is a magnificent blend of originating, *eros* (Greek word for love), genital, and the Latin present form of the verb erect; the idea combines in one word the connection between building and the creative aspect of the sexual act. The overtones of height in the last part are suggested by such words as *waalworth*, *eyeful*, *hoyth*, *entowerly*, *skyerscape*, and *himals* (German Himmel, high, and Himalayas), until they reach a climax in *hierarchitecti-tiptitoploftical*:

Bygmester Finnegan, of the Stuttering Hand, freemen's maurer, lived in the broadest way immarginable in his rushlit toofarback for messuages before joshuan judges had given us numbers or Helviticus committed deuteronomy (one yeastyday he sternely struxk his tete in a tub for to watsch the future of his fates but ere he swiftly stook it out again, by the might of moses, the very water was eviparated and all the guennesses had met their exodus so that ought to show you what a pentschanjeuchy chap he was!) and during mighty odd years this man of hod, cement and edifices in Toper's Thorp piled buildung supra buildung pon the banks for the livers by the Soangso. He addle liddle phifie Annie ugged the little craythur. Wither hayre in honds tuck up your part inher. Oftwhile balbulous, mithre ahead, with goodly trowel in grasp and ivoroiled overalls which he habitacularly fondseed, like Haroun Childeric Eggeberth he would caligulate by multiplicables the alltitude and malltitude until he seesaw by neatlight of the liquor wheretwin 'twas born, his roundhead staple of other days to rise in undress maisonry upstanded (joygrantit!) a waalworth of a skyerscape of most eyeful hoyth entowerly, erigenating from next to nothing and celescalating the himals and all, hierarchitectitiptitop-loftical, with a burning bush abob off its baubletop and with larrons o'toolers clittering up and tombles a'buckets clottering down.[2]

Even with this lengthy explanation, not all the connotations of the passage are explained. For example, *Bygmester* sounds like "big Mr. Finnegan" and suggests the Scandinavian word for builder (compare German *Baumeister*); *yeastyday* suggests yesterday and the never ceasing fermenting quality of yeast; *eviparated* suggests evaporated and the Latin words meaning era and prepare; *pentaschanjeuchy* suggests the Pentateuch, the first five books of the Old Testament, the antics of a Punch-and-Judy show, and perhaps the Sanskrit *Panchatantra*; *buildung* suggests building and German *Bildung*, or imagination; *alltitude* suggests altitude and all; and so on. There is also a suggestion in the whole pas-

[2] *Ibid.*, 4.

sage of the Tower of Babel legend that is echoed in the blasphemous and futile attempt of the giants to build a tower to reach Heaven. The miraculous burning bush of Moses crowns the lofty edifice, while the Irish saint, Lawrence O'Toole, and the English saint, Thomas à Becket, pass each other going up and down in the buckets used to hoist supplies.

This is a long explanation for one passage, and yet it contains only some of those connotations that are explained by my experience. Another reader might get more, or come out with a different interpretation. The process, however, is plain enough, for it is the final step in Joyce's lifelong pursuit of words in which he startles us and makes us see the whole of life in a new light. The process began with the artist as a young man in search of new styles and became perfected, as far as ordinary conventional language could go, in the infinite variety of *Ulysses*. In *Finnegans Wake*, the process tries to change language itself and reaches its logical conclusion—or an impasse. Here the linguist must stop, and the critic take over.

Finnegans Wake is too new to be thoroughly understood; Joyce did not work seventeen years on a trifle to be read overnight. But the style presents an aesthetic problem that many have pondered but seldom practiced: to what extent can literature approach music? I can only suggest a possible answer by giving my own reactions to this new technique. Where I am familiar with the fused ideas the result is very pleasing, for it does what the best poetry has always done: it creates a brave new world of images by lifting new words and pulling the old shells of accumulated semantic tradition off the old words. Shakespeare and Milton, among English poets, were particularly good at this renewing of language. Joyce did it, too, in *Ulysses*, by his unerring choice of words and his invention of startling compounds. But here he breaks with tradition altogether, creates strange words, and builds up from them polysemantic associations based upon prodigious reading, upon a knowledge of several languages, and upon a multitude of local allusions that only Dubliners of a certain era understand in full.

It is upon this last point that I find Joyce's virtuosity annoying. Music is universal because, if it is well performed, it can be understood without respect to linguistic barriers. But literature cannot be divorced from meaning, and a given word does not mean the same thing to an Englishman, a Frenchman, and a German, no matter how much you change it. Joyce may expect the intelligent reader to know these three languages and even throw in a little Latin and less Greek, but how can he expect to include Russian, Gaelic, and the Scandinavian languages? Most of us know our nursery rimes, proverbs, snatches of Shakespeare and the Bible, and Aesop's fables, but few of us are familiar with Dublin's suburbs or with the music-hall songs of decades ago.

Perhaps no one can understand all of it. There is such plenty that I can take part of it and still come away enriched by the experience. Whether Joyce has gone too far remains to be seen. He has, I believe, pushed the analogy between music and poetry as far as it can safely be carried. In the hands of a less capable stylist, however, it might easily become bathos, and one can imagine that his intelligent followers will temper the style and make it over for the average reader as they did with the stream of consciousness in *Ulysses*.

Let me close with a bit of advice in the reading of Joyce,

especially *Finnegans Wake:* relax—get over the idea that it is a grim business and enjoy yourself. "Actually," says Harry Levin, one of Joyce's best critics, "it is a wonderful game—by no means a private affair, but one in which many may join, each with his own contribution, and the more the merrier." To a lover of words it is exciting. Its method is not too different from that used in solving a crossword puzzle in *The London Times Weekly,* yet its goal is an understanding of the problems of life and death. The problem is linguistic as well as aesthetic, and in recent years it has attracted the attention of sympathetic philologists. With their help we may in time learn to separate the wheat from the chaff, the choice from the steins.

aðvice on further reaðing about joyce

I am not as bold today as I was in 1955 about giving advice to the general reader. New books on Joyce are published at the rate of about one a month, and many articles about him appear in learned journals all over the world, two of which, the *James Joyce Quarterly* and *A Wake Newslitter*, are devoted entirely to his work. A fairly complete listing is given in the annual MLA International Bibliography; of the 83 items which appeared in 1966 and the 145 which appeared in 1967, most are brief notes, but many are long critical articles, and 10 to 12 for each year are books, dissertations, or collections of essays.

At the present rate of acceleration, Joyce scholarship will soon engulf even the specialist. Surely the time for synthesis has arrived, the time for good Joyce scholars to evaluate the accumulation, even as Marvin Magalaner and Richard Kain did in 1956 with *Joyce: The Man, the Work, the Reputation*. Good analytical bibliographies like Joseph Prescott's in *Configurations* and the "Selected Checklist" in *Modern Fiction Studies* for Spring, 1969, are helpful.

In recent years have appeared some very valuable books on Joyce that even the general reader cannot afford to miss. Richard Ellmann published his definitive biography, *James Joyce*, in 1959 and his edition of the letters in 1966. The ultimate recognition of

Joyce as an important writer came when J. I. M. Stewart included him among the eight writers chosen to represent the twentieth century in the Oxford History of English Literature series: "Whether Joyce is in fact to be convicted of progressive artistic irresponsibility is a very hard question. But even if he is he remains, at least as a writer's writer, a very important figure indeed." (Stewart's bibliography, incidentally, is the excellent guide we have learned to expect from the Oxford History in the form of brief critical comment on the most important books.)

Of the general criticism which has appeared since 1955, W. Y. Tindall brings to his *Reader's Guide to James Joyce* (1959) the critical acumen of his earlier book (*James Joyce*, 1950). Admittedly a student's guide, the work has outstanding chapters on *Portrait of the Artist* and *Finnegans Wake*. Joseph Prescott's *Exploring James Joyce* (1964) has excellent essays, especially the one on Molly Bloom, but we still await the analysis of *Ulysses* that Prescott has been promising for many years. Harry Blamires's *The Bloomsday Book: A Guide Through Joyce's* Ulysses (1966), which is a retelling of the story page by page, should prove helpful, and Anthony Burgess's *ReJoyce* (1965), a direct approach to Joyce's writings, combines delightful style with sensitive criticism.

Advanced readers will find much of value in Hugh Kenner's *Dublin's Joyce* (1965), S. L. Goldberg's *The Classical Temper* (1961), and R. M. Adams's *Surface and Symbol* (1962), the last two being critical studies in depth of *Ulysses*. A. W. Litz's *The Art of James Joyce* (1960; revised paperback, 1963) is an important critical study based on various texts of *Ulysses* and *Finnegans Wake*.

For advanced readers of *Finnegans Wake* the criticism of Clive Hart and Bernard Benstock is recommended, as well as the specialized explications by J. S. Atherton, F. M. Boldereff, M. J. C. Hodgart, Fritz Senn, and many others. The exciting evolution of the infinite invention employed in composing the book has been culled from the voluminous and baffling notebooks in the British Museum and libraries of Buffalo, Yale, and Cornell by David Hayman (*A First-Draft Version of Finnegans Wake,* 1962), *Anna Livia Plurabelle: The Making of a Chapter* (1960), edited by Fred Higginson, *James Joyce's Scribbledehobble: The Ur-Workbook for Finnegans Wake* (1961), edited by Thomas E. Connolly, and Stanley Sutton's ambitious *The Argument of Ulysses* (1964) are difficult for the beginning reader, who, brave soul, will do better with selections from Tindall, Benstock, Hart, and *Second Census of Finnegans Wake,* by Adaline Glasheen (1963).

The standard bibliography is still that of Slocum and Cahoon (1953). For critical and secondary studies, see the list of R. H. Deming (1964) and the annual Modern Language Association bibliographies for subsequent years.

inδex

Addison, Joseph: 114
AE (George William Russell): 56, 145
Alliteration, Joyce's use of: 110
Archaic diction, Joyce's use of: 110
Astrology: 101
Autobiography, Joyce's real: 9–10

Baake, Josef: 140n.
Beaconsfield, Lord: 127
Beaumont and Fletcher: 112
Beowulf: 110
Berlitz School, Trieste: 10
Bible: early translation of, 111; King James, 112
Blake, William: 113
Bowling, L. E.: 48n.
Browne, Thomas: 112, 113
Budgen, Frank: 108
Bunyan, John: 112
Burke, Edmund: 114
Burton, Robert: 113
Byron, Lord: 127

Carlyle, Thomas: 117
Celtic renaissance: 77

Richards, Grant: 10, 11, 24
Richardson, Samuel: 114
Roman Catholic Church: 34–35, 145
Ruskin, John: 116
Russell, George William: *see* AE